West Midlands Vol I

Edited by Steve Twelvetree

Young Writers
First published in Great Britain in 2004 by:
Young Writers
Remus House
Coltsfoot Drive
Peterborough
PE2 9JX
Telephone: 01733 890066
Website: www.youngwriters.co.uk

SB ISBN 1 84460 497 7

Foreword

Young Writers was established in 1991 and has been passionately devoted to the promotion of reading and writing in children and young adults ever since. The quest continues today. Young Writers remains as committed to engendering the fostering of burgeoning poetic and literary talent as ever.

This year's Young Writers competition has proven as vibrant and dynamic as ever and we are delighted to present a showcase of the best poetry from across the UK. Each poem has been carefully selected from a wealth of *Once Upon A Rhyme* entries before ultimately being published in this, our twelfth primary school poetry series.

Once again, we have been supremely impressed by the overall high quality of the entries we have received. The imagination, energy and creativity which has gone into each young writer's entry made choosing the best poems a challenging and often difficult but ultimately hugely rewarding task - the general high standard of the work submitted amply vindicating this opportunity to bring their poetry to a larger appreciative audience.

We sincerely hope you are pleased with our final selection and that you will enjoy *Once Upon A Rhyme West Midlands Vol I* for many years to come.

Contents

St Alphege CE Junior School, Solihull

St Nicholas RC School, Sutton Coldfield

The Poems

The Snowy Day

There's sparkling snow all down the road,
Lots of snowballs swirling,
A white blanket of white glittery balls,
Chimney tops covered with soft ice,
Robins singing, waking us up,
No sun shining in the winter,
Children in gloves and woolly jumpers,
Snowflakes glazing,
Trees shaken by the cold, roaring wind,
Children shouting, playing in the snow,
Making a snowman, oh, that's a show,
People marching along the slippery path.

Kirsty Green (8)

Whatif?

(Based on 'Whatif' by Shel Silverstein)

'Last night, while I lay thinking here,
Some whatifs crawled inside my ear
And pranced and partied all night long
And sang their old whatif song:'
Whatif I lost my shoe?
Whatif I fell in dog poo?
Whatif I'm late for school?
Whatif I fall in the swimming pool?
Whatif there are animals in the class?
Whatif I fell in glass?
Whatif my skirt fell down?
Whatif I turn into a clown?

'Everything seems so swell and then . . .

The whatifs strike again!'

Elizabeth Arnold (10)
Amblecote Primary School

Whatif?

(Based on 'Whatif' by Shel Silverstein)

Whatif I don't do my best?
Whatif I miss the test?
Whatif I don't score a goal?
Whatif I don't get a pet mole?
Whatif I am late?
Whatif I lose my mate?
Whatif I lose my head?
Whatif I don't go to bed?
Whatif I lose my pup?
Whatif I hiccup?
Whatif I lose my house?
Whatif I live with a mouse?
Whatif I miss school?
Whatif I drowned in a pool?

Kieran Pope (9)
Amblecote Primary School

Pollution, Pollution

Pollution spreads like butter on bread,
It flows through the beautiful river,
Killing everything in its path . . .

Toxic fumes are in the air,
We breathe it in, it's not fair -
It flows to the glittering sea
And it kills the fish as you can see . . .

A ship can crash into a rock
And all the fish will suffer and drop -
We go on holiday on a plane,
It drops fumes and we start again . . .

If you block its path you will be taken
And it doesn't give you time to explain.

Edward Shrimpton (11)
Amblecote Primary School

Whatif?

(Based on 'Whatif' by Shel Silverstein)

'Last night, while I lay thinking here,
Some whatifs crawled inside my ear
And pranced and partied all night long
And sang old whatif songs:'
Whatif I turn up late for school?
Whatif I fall in the swimming pool?
Whatif I bang heads in school?
Whatif I get sick and I die?
Whatif the mobiles fall down?
Whatif I don't get a crown?
Whatif the school is on fire?
Whatif my dad has not got a tyre?
'Everything seems swell and then
The night-time whatifs strike again!'

Rebecca Jones (10)
Amblecote Primary School

Whatif?

(Based on 'Whatif' by Shel Silverstein)

Whatif I don't do my best?
Whatif I don't do my test?
Whatif I don't score my goal?
Whatif I don't have a pet mole?
Whatif I'm really late?
Whatif I lose my mate?
Whatif I lose my head?
Whatif I go to bed?
Whatif I lose my cup?
Whatif I hiccup?

Matthew Heath (9)
Amblecote Primary School

Pollution

There's pollution in the air,
Pollution in the sea,
It's everywhere!
Gases and toxic fumes,
We breathe it in,
Just not fair!
Power stations blacking the sky,
So the acid rain burns the trees,
Killing the wildlife as it goes,
There's pollution in the air,
Pollution in the sea,
Not fair!

There's big, black toxic fumes
Belching out,
The power stations are choking birds,
It's everywhere,
Not fair!

James Rawlings (10)
Amblecote Primary School

Best Friends

Gee and D are the best of mates,
They are always smashing plates.

Their favourite food is macaroni cheese,
Can we have some more please?

They ride their BMXs all day long,
But when they get back, they're a bit of a pong!

Game Boy SP is fun to play,
I could play it every day!

George Gee (9)
Amblecote Primary School

My Enchanted Food

Fairy cakes, bubble bakes,
Sugar shakes and castle cakes.

Enchanted food is good to eat,
It makes you feel very, very sweet.

Fairy cakes are yummy to eat,
The feeling goes right down to your feet.

Bubble bakes are full of fun
And leaves a nice feeling in your tum.

Sugar shakes are full of laughter,
You can't remember anything after.

Castle cakes are best of all
With chocolate filling although rather small.

Here is some more enchanted food,
Brace yourself you might get in a mood.

Dead marshmallow ants,
Slide up and down your throat till you choke.

Wet weeping mice
That taste like lice

And now for a dish that's a real treat,
Saucy mice with salted feet.

Hope you like my menu for enchanted food,
If you do, just give me a call

And ask for Jude, I will send you a dish fit for a king
And I promise you it will make you sing.

Harriet Pickett (9)
Amblecote Primary School

Pollution!

On the planet we live,
There's lots of litter and waste,
Petrol, oil and toxic fumes,
Makes it a horrible place.

On the planet we live,
The graffiti and gases like CO_2,
Pollute our Earth,
Then where will we live?

On the planet we live,
There is poisonous waste everywhere,
Toxic, human and animal waste
Is growing everywhere.

On the planet we live,
Pollution is growing all around us,
In the sea and on the land;
Spreads this horrible potion.

On the planet we live,
The pollution is getting worse,
The animals are dying off
And no longer is this a healthy Earth.

Emily White (10)
Amblecote Primary School

Friendship

Friendship is about caring and being kind,
Playing games is so fun!
We do exciting stuff,
Friendship is the best, never have enough!
Friendship is about being happy and being glad,
Being together is so cool!
We like sharing and giving,
Friendship is so fab!

Olivia Tulloch (8)
Amblecote Primary School

Hearing Noises

Walking in the woods,
By the riverbank,
Heard a rattle,
Turned around,
A snake!
I shivered.

Walking in the woods,
Under thick trees,
Heard a gentle tap,
Turned around,
A spider!
I screamed.

Walking in the woods,
Down by the caves,
Heard a screech,
Turned around,
A bat!
I ran.

Oliver Goode (11)
Amblecote Primary School

Friendship

A ypril is my best friend
Y oung and sweet and smart
P robably caring deep down in her heart
R eally she is very talented but she doesn't show it
I want her to be my friend
L oving, caring Aypril.

Abigail Weaver (8)
Amblecote Primary School

The Water Fairies

There is something wrong with the magic pool
A magic spell has made it cool
'Do not worry,' squeaked the mice
'We'll tell Mr Owl we'll be back in a trice.'
'Mr Owl has invited King Oberon to his house,' said Queen Mouse

So when the day had turned to night
King Oberon lit a bright light
And flew to Mr Owl
Who wrapped King Oberon in a towel
'You need to find the magic jewel
That has the power to melt the pool'
So off the little mice did scurry
To Gold Mountain in a hurry
In no time the jewel was found
And soon the water fairies were swimming around.

Eleanor Hickman Jones (8)
Amblecote Primary School

Pollution

Boom! Boom! Boom! goes the music -
No one turns it down . . .
Spray! Spray! Spray! goes grimy graffiti -
No one seems to frown.
Everybody thinks it's OK,
No one seems to care . . .
If we don't stop this worldwide killer,
It just won't be fair.
Purple paint fumes on the street;
Rubbish at my flimsy feet . . .
If we stop this dastardly disaster;
Animals will not die faster . . .

Mark Clement (10)
Amblecote Primary School

Snake

A snake
glides
through
grass
over
pebbles

Forked
tongue never
speaking

But its
body
whispers
listen . . .

Adil Karim (10)
Amblecote Primary School

A Rose

There is a
Flower down the bottom
Of the garden,
Red as a rose,
The centre is as big
As a baseball,
Two small buds
With long leaves
And a bendy stem
With little thorns,
No friends,
A rose all alone.

Chelsea Wilkes (10)
Amblecote Primary School

Whatif

(Based on 'Whatif' By Shel Silverstein)

'Last night, while I lay thinking here,
Some whatifs crawled inside my ear
And pranced and partied all night long
And sang their same old whatif song.'
Whatif I turned up late for school?
Whatif I fall into the swimming pool?
Whatif I hurt myself?
Whatif I had bad health?
Whatif my shirt got ripped?
Whatif I got dipped?
'Everything seems swell and then
The night-time whatifs strike again!'

Charlotte Cartwright (10)
Amblecote Primary School

The Polluted World

In the flats; on the walls it stays,
On the bus; on the seats it sticks,
In the sea; on the top it floats,
In the jungle; in the air it kills - it kills.

On the beach; in the sand it hurts,
On the street; in the sky it's loud.
In the flats, the bus, the sea and the jungle,
On the beach and especially on the street,
It kills and it kills, but do we do anything about it?
No!

Charlotte Bowman (10)
Amblecote Primary School

Pollution

No one can stand the noise
Of graffiti drawn by boys,
Humans dropping litter
Making our world bitter.

Unfortunately animals are dying,
The wildlife of animals
Or their habitats,
Polluting the world
Means polluting poor,
We're so selfish,
Don't we care anymore?

Cigarette ends,
Crisp packets,
Trolleys or baskets,
Who will we blame?
Ourselves of course!

Barrels of oil in the ocean,
We could make a potion,
There's something in the air,
It travels everywhere.

It pollutes the seas,
It pollutes the trees,
It could be acid rain,
It could be poison,
Meanwhile it's polluting the world,
It will carry on forever and ever.

Natasha Osborne (10)
Amblecote Primary School

Pollution

Pollution here,
Pollution there,
Pollution's killing everywhere!
Around the world, as you go.
Pollution lurks in sea, sand and snow!
It kills and kills again,
Animals and their den.
Pollution is everywhere,
Over here and over there!
Innocent lives are being taken,
It lurks around the world.
Understand you must . . .
The world is being taken!
It kills everything
In its path,
Only you and me can stop it,
No, it's not fair, but it's our fault!
Pollution in the sea,
Pollution in the air,
Pollution is spreading everywhere!
Are we going to get cleaner
Or simply just meaner?
Pollution kills animals,
Birds, reptiles and mammals!
If you look very carefully,
You will see,
Pollution effects everyone,
Including you and me!
Pollution kills!
Stop it now!

Kiran Jagpal (11)
Amblecote Primary School

Too Many To Count

There are too many
Too many to count
Badgers hollowing out the Earth
Foxes hunting
Birds chanting
Fishes leaping in and out
Too many to count
Pintos cantering
Deer grazing
Snakes hissing
Baby birds hatching
Too many to count
Squirrels tracing nuts
Mice scurrying
Birds of prey lurking
Rabbits capering
Too many to count
But all animals big or small
Growing and dying
So take care of them all
Or soon there won't be
Too many to count!

Charlie Smith (11)
Amblecote Primary School

The Beach

Everybody can see the big blue ocean,
Sweeping over the sandy beach,
Collecting shells,
Making sandcastles,
Swimming in the silvery sea.

Ben James (10)
Amblecote Primary School

Pollution

P ollution is everywhere,
O ver here and over there,
L urking in your house,
L ooking for a new home to stay,
U nder the ground it digs down deep,
T he world is being polluted,
I t is killing everything,
O n and on it grows, bigger and bigger,
N o one will stop it until it's too late.
Pollution kills!

Cheryl Bloomfield (11)
Amblecote Primary School

Pollution!

Deadly gas lurking through treetops,
Destroying birds as they sing,
Newborn chicks as they hatch,
. . . *The gas kills!*

Litter dropping in greenish water,
It drops, splatters and falls,
It pollutes in streams, rivers, reservoirs and lakes,
. . . *The litter kills!*

Faye Espley (11)
Amblecote Primary School

The Seaside

Horses on sand galloping softly,
Sea bright aqua with white,
Children running on the smooth silvery sand,
Divers watching dolphins in deep oceans,
Dashing out to sea on a big black speedboat
. . . Is fun!

Holli Rudall (11)
Amblecote Primary School

I Run In The Fields

I run in the fields and feel glad,
I feel free picking mushrooms,
Hearing them go bang,
Swimming in a lake,
Take me to another level.

The water circles like a Ferris wheel,
I feel happy climbing tall trees,
Fishing, running in nature,
It's fun to me.

Christopher Homer (11)
Amblecote Primary School

I Like . . .

I like climbing trees to see a lovely view,
Picking wonderful flowers but only the fabulous blue,
I love running through grey greenish grass,
Playing on snowy, sparkly ground.
I like to see the grey squirrels,
I love to kick the leaves in the gutter,
I like to run on the sandy beaches,
I love walking by the sweeping black river,
It really is . . .
Superb!

Thomas Hadlington (11)
Amblecote Primary School

Night-Time

I went to bed one cloudy night,
It was cold and damp and windy too,
Trees were blowing and leaves were swooshing,
Round and round the cloudy air.

Sara Dakin (10)
Amblecote Primary School

Animals In The Day

High in the trees birds sing,
Newborn chicks learn to fly,
Squirrels pounce from tree to tree,
Chattering as they leap.

Fish leap in and out of water,
Trying to reach the sun.
Frogs jump in and out of water,
Laying frogspawn.

Mice are hiding to keep alive,
Foxes are hunting too,
It's mice they really want,
To feed their young and chew.

Rabbits are burrowing for a place to rest,
Deer calm down for the night.
Everybody goes to sleep,
While the sun's down and the moon's up.

Giorgia Johnson (11)
Amblecote Primary School

Running Through Long Grass

Running through long grass is a very fun thing to do
Jumping into the air
To catch green slimy grasshoppers
Slithering snakes slide up the grimy rocks

The bees nest to produce sticky honey
The horses gallop in the long green grass
Tortoises walk to find water
Everybody walks in the long green grass
It's fun . . .

Natalie Farnsworth (11)
Amblecote Primary School

What's Happening

What's happening to the playground?
There are smells in the air,
It makes you hear a sound,
It makes you stop and stare!

What's happening to the river?
It's cloudy with oil,
It's killing all of the fish,
It's like tinfoil!

What's happening to the park?
There is dog waste on the floor,
This is not how it should be,
What are the bins for?

What's wrong with our world?
It's like a pigsty,
Help the world be a better place,
Please, please help me!

Sophie Charles (11)
Amblecote Primary School

Playing In The Woods

Playing in the woods,
Running and jumping in puddles.
Playing in the woods,
Hiding behind trees.
Playing in the woods,
Making huge leaf piles.
Playing in the woods,
Scattering leaves everywhere!
Playing in the woods
. . . Is fun!

Benjamin Tustin (11)
Amblecote Primary School

The Animals' Cry

Lots of dolphins drifting along . . .
Very merrily singing a song,
But then one dolphin started to cry,
The cause caught the other dolphin's eye,
'Look at that above us floating in the sea,
I don't think we should eat it, it doesn't look like food to me!'

The horse is merrily trotting along,
Until he treads in something strong,
His hoof is caught . . .
In a crisp packet that was bought,
Left on the ground!
Destroying the world all around!

A flock of birds hovering along,
Breathing terrible things into their lungs,
Because pollution is in the air!
Not just in the air, *everywhere!*

So what have we done to this Earth?
Is pollution all it is worth?
So I guess there is just one thing to say,
Pollution kills in every way

Emily Langridge (10)
Amblecote Primary School

Playing In The Park

I am going to have fun today,
If all my friends come out to play,
We will go swimming and to the park
And we will stay until it gets dark.
We'll pick daisies in the park
And link them in beautiful chains.
If we have time we'll feed the ducks,
Then climb up and down the climbing frames.

Kirsty Pearson (11)
Amblecote Primary School

In The Deep Dark Wood

In the deep dark wood . . .
Snakes slither,
Moles dither.
Birds circle, prey and wait,
Foxes play in the rain.

In the deep dark wood . . .
Bugs fly high in the sky,
Butterflies float so high they disappear,
Wild birds sing and cheep.

In the deep dark wood . . .
Nature moves,
Birds fly,
Frogs jump,
Bugs crawl,
Snakes slither,
Moles dig.

In the deep dark wood . . .
Nature is everywhere, don't ruin it for them.

Amy Kelly (10)
Amblecote Primary School

I Go To The Woods

I go to the woods
And see butterflies flying,
The birds fly around,
I look behind me,
A bird lands on my head,
I walk down the path
And see horses grazing
And see rabbits beneath them,
Then I jump on a horse
And ride home.

Jamie Pope (11)
Amblecote Primary School

Pollution Everywhere

Go out on the street,
Litter everywhere,
Oil on the paths,
No one seems to care.

Music exploding out,
Someone turn it down,
If we don't stop this killer,
Someone will frown.

Go out in the car,
You will see,
That everywhere
Could annihilate me.

Just conjure up if pollution goes,
Will we be able to breathe?
Who knows!

Laura Green (10)
Amblecote Primary School

Journeys

I'd love to explore . . .
The dark, steamy jungle
And watch tigers and snakes
Hunt for prey

I'd love to explore . . .
The wet, green forest
And watch beautiful birds
Fly around

I'd love to explore . . .
The long, sandy beaches
And watch colourful boats
Sail on the bright blue sea

I'd love to explore!

Kyle Drew (11)
Amblecote Primary School

Pollution

Pollution is a gas called carbon dioxide
It's like an oil or petrol
It's old things not used
It makes boats crash and oil splash

There are fish in the sea -
But what about me?
We're going down a sewer -
But what can you see?

Me in the water or the sea . . .
In the water there are fish
Don't kill them
Give them to me
I'll think what to do
I could stick them in a tank
Where they get stuck
Don't pollute the air anymore
Because it's already killing things like animals
Please stop it and hurry up.

Lee Russon (10)
Amblecote Primary School

Pollution!

Pollution has come,
Oil dripping from . . .
Lorries and trucks,
Lots of fumes,
Under the ground,
There is something in the sewage,
It is everywhere,
Over the world it's spreading,
(No more *pollution* please!)

Steven Bidmead (10)
Amblecote Primary School

What Is It? Is It Pollution?

There's oil in the river and it will get me soon,
I'm sure it will get me before the moon,
The trees are all dying, I know and I can't see,
Everyone's crying, but of course not me,
The sea smells horrible,
It's dark and dull,
There's also car parts in the sea,
So if you can please, please help me,
Pollution's all around the world,
I know and I can't see,
It's even all curled and twirled,
So if you can please just help me,
Pollution's killing me,
So help, help, help,
If you can take it away,
Then we can get back to a nice normal day.

Emma Guest (11)
Amblecote Primary School

Pollution

In the seas, oceans and waters
There are oils spreading into these
Different kinds of waters,
It may be the cars that zoom fast,
Past these incredible waters,
It's a shame if animals die
From the oils and rubbish.
Do you know what some people do
When they go past in boats?
You can be poisoning these wonderful oceans
And seas with toxic fumes,
People will be sighing and crying,
If these creatures die in the oceans and seas,
Please don't throw junk
Into these waters, it's a shame!

Emma Goodall (10)
Amblecote Primary School

The Killer Nightmare

Graffiti is everywhere you look,
This colourful masterpiece,
Destroys everything it touches,
As a car engine starts,
Out come the fumes,
You choke as you breathe it in . . .
When you smoke
You make other innocent people smoke too,
A crisp packet is dropped
And a small, harmless animal is trapped,
We shall all be . . . ensnared, captured,
If we don't stop this killer!

Chloe Jagpal (11)
Amblecote Primary School

Pollution

Pollution
Is like a lotion
All the fish are dying
And people are still crying
The rainforests are going
And rubbish is still growing
Graffiti is killing
And people's lives are spilling
Pollution must stop because
It kills and it kills and it kills
So we might move in space
To continue the human race
Stop it now!

Rhys Smith (10)
Amblecote Primary School

Pollution!

Pollution drifts, floats
And sticks to everything in its path,
It kills everything in its path,
Oil lies on top of the sea
Killing fish and whales,
However it washes up on the beach
Killing crabs and turtles.
Chewing gum
Stuck to the footpaths,
Also on the roads,
Blue, white and green everywhere you go.
Graffiti sprayed on the walls,
Different colours, gang logos and for fun,
Crisp packets fluttering in the wind,
Dropped on the ground.
Cars driving along,
Leaving only smoke behind them.
Plants soaking up oil and petrol.
We have polluted the world,
We have to
Live with it.

Christopher Mills (11)
Amblecote Primary School

Winter

As the day starts, the ground is white,
The snow has fallen during the night,
Families going down on skis,
While snow is falling from the trees,
Ice frozen to the ground,
As the ducks skate around,
Trees covered in snow,
As the sun makes the ice glow,
As the sun comes up to play,
All the snow goes away.

Lloyd Smith (10)
Bentley Heath Primary School

Winter Warm

On a winter's night,
All warm and snug,
Wrapped up tight,
Fire burning warm.

All asleep,
Dreaming of a white Christmas,
Footprints printed,
In white gleaming snow.

Grass turned to hard crystal,
Cold breezes blowing in the air quietly,
Snow gently falling,
Snowflakes made in shapes.

Wake in the morning all excited,
Excited that Santa has come,
Open all your presents,
You don't want Christmas to be done.

Serena Dhak (9)
Bentley Heath Primary School

Winter

Children playing in the snow
Snow-topped trees fill the sky
Snow gleaming on the lake
While birds sing in the trees
Sledges whizzing down hills
While people cover themselves in snow
As the day comes to an end
People go back to their cosy beds
In the night
The moon glistening over the town
While children sleep tight.

Eloise Barker (9)
Bentley Heath Primary School

Animals Of The Winter

In the moonlight
The cats are prowling
Snow is falling
Kittens are sleeping
In the moonlight
The foxes are prowling
Ready to catch their prey

In the early morning
When the bunnies are hopping
And the dogs are chasing
The sun will rise

In the late afternoon
When the horses are galloping
And the birds are flying
The sun goes down.

Lucy Venner (9)
Bentley Heath Primary School

In The Darkness Of The Night

In the darkness of the night
Mice scurry in the moonlight
You can see the silver gleam
As you watch the silver stream

You can see the wavy sea
Watching dolphins jump gracefully
Silently sleeps the little dog
Sleeping as still as a log.

Kirsty Smitten (9)
Bentley Heath Primary School

Rhonda

Rhonda loves cheddar cheese,
She'll eat a pound of it if you please.
Rhonda has a squeaky bone,
But now she won't leave it alone.
Rhonda is brown and white,
Sometimes she gives you a fright.
Rhonda eats yoghurt pots,
Every day lots and lots.
Rhonda loves sticks
And she loves doing tricks.
Rhonda is furry and soft,
She loves sleeping in the loft.
Rhonda is very shy,
So from me and Rhonda bye-bye.

Georgina Russell (10)
Bentley Heath Primary School

Socks

Socks is a cat
She loves people giving her a pat
She loves eating delicious meat
And loves licking her white feet
When people stroke her fur
She gives you a quiet soft purr
When it is hot, Socks bathes in the sun
And jumps on people just for fun
Socks is a very old cat
And I love her very much.

Elizabeth Arnold (9)
Bentley Heath Primary School

The Mare

Walking in the forest,
When I see a mare,
The moonlight glinting,
On her silver-dappled hair.

Neighing softly,
A foal by her side,
Her mother watching,
Filled with pride.

The trees surrounding them,
Like a brick wall,
Keeping them from danger,
Sweeping high and tall.

They'll always be in the forest,
Standing there together,
They'll always have each other,
Forever and ever.

Rhiannon Reynolds (10)
Bentley Heath Primary School

The Wind

I'm invisible
But noisy
I circle around you
You don't know my next trick
I work all day and night
Next I might blow a tree down
Or pull your hair
I might not have arms or legs
But . . . *beware!*

Victoria Berrey (9)
Bentley Heath Primary School

Volcano

On the top of a mountain in Scotland,
Sat a volcano that could erupt;
The lava inside was boiling orange,
Climbing the outside was tough.

The people in the town below,
All hid way in their bungalows;
Soon the volcano is sure to erupt,
The orange lava trickles down.

The orange sea floods the town,
Melting all things around;
The thud of trees as they hit the ground,
That's the end of the little town.

Ali Walker (10)
Bentley Heath Primary School

My Friend, Tiger

Tiger the cat,
Has a big black toy rat,
He runs up and down trees
And chases the birds and bees,
Tiger gives a big purr
If you tickle his fur,
He climbs on my bed,
Then rests on my head,
A dish of his favourite food,
Always puts him in a good mood,
So that's the story of my best mate.

Rachel Quinney (10)
Bentley Heath Primary School

When Spring Comes

When spring comes does anyone care
About the dew just lying there
Or about the bunnies hopping around
Or birds' footsteps making no sound?

When spring comes does anyone care
About the squirrel with its innocent stare
Or about the daffodils opening up
Or a hedgehog sniffing a buttercup?

When spring comes does anyone care
About a cold, hungry mare
Or about the buds all newborn
Or a fox cub from its mother torn?

Grace Kneafsey (10)
Bentley Heath Primary School

Melly, My Baby Sister

Melly my baby sister is really funny
She runs around and does somersaults
But only when it's sunny!
She's really small
Most people think she's cool
She loves sweets
And smiles to everyone she meets
Melly's such a chatterbox
But she's my sister
And I love her lots!

Faye Lawless (9)
Bentley Heath Primary School

Dolphins Playing

Dolphins playing happily with each other
Baby dolphin swimming along with its mother
Jumping up from the water into the midnight sky
Soon a whale comes by

Their grey skin shimmering in the water
The mother squeaks at her daughter
Their big blue eyes filling with happiness
In the water without any loneliness

The water glistening as they play
While the other dolphins make their way
The dolphins play with their friends
The dolphins' day never ends!

Danielle Hancock (9)
Bentley Heath Primary School

My Poem About Sam

I love my cat,
He's big and fat.
His colour's black
And he's everyone's cat.
He loves his food,
But gets in a mood.
He loves his fuss,
But he's still my puss.

Chloe Gardner (10)
Bentley Heath Primary School

Dragon Of The Sky

Dragon of the sky,
He has a glint of bright red in his eye.
He flies swiftly through the air
And lives down on the reef by the sea.
He's full of curiosity,
He's stronger than 50 men,
A giant cave is his den.
Look up into the bright starry night,
What a sight you'll see,
It's the dragon of the sky.

Tomas Hallett (10)
Bentley Heath Primary School

Horses Of A Winter's Night

Moonlight rays beaming down,
Creating faint dapples on creatures that make no sound;
As they swiftly flee, their hooves thudding softly on the frosty ground,
They silently slide to a halt, ears pricked, heads held high.

Their eyes shining out of the darkness,
Through the boughs of the tender willow,
Restlessly pawing the ground,
Snowflakes falling as they disappear,
The horses of the winter.

Katherine Burdon (9)
Bentley Heath Primary School

Beach Debate

The beach is a happy place,
Sun and fun,
The sea talks
To the golden sand,
The sun gleams
Through the fluffy clouds.

The beach is a sad place,
Crisp packets crunch underfoot,
The rats crawl down through the sand,
People crowd to get in,
The children can't play.

Sam Mather (9)
Bentley Heath Primary School

Think

Think of someone who has unfortunately died
Think of someone who has sadly cried
Think of something you have lost
When you were playing in the frost

Think when you die will there be birds in the sky?
Think will you be here in 12 years
Or will some people be shedding their tears?
Think will you still love and cherish your mum
Even when she has gone?

Lizzie Russell (9)
Bentley Heath Primary School

Winter

In the morning, snow is falling,
Snow-topped trees and frosted leaves.

Skiddy ground and whizzy kids,
Snowball fights in the trees.

Footprints frosted in the snow,
Snowmen melting in the sun.

The snow is glistening on the ground,
The snow is swirling round and round.

Francesca O'Keeffe (9)
Bentley Heath Primary School

Tortoise

The tortoise moves very slowly,
His legs are very short,
He won the race,
Against the hare,
The hare's lesson was taught.

From today, the hare has learnt,
The tortoise was alright,
All is happy,
The end has come,
You'll never see such a happy sight.

Rebecca Winters (9)
Bentley Heath Primary School

Falling Snow

Glittery snow falls and falls
As Jack Frost paints pictures on our windows
Then children wake up, peep out the window
For a look
As the snow crunches under their feet
The glittery snow still falling down
Snow angels get painted on the ground
When the sun comes up ice starts dripping
Dripping, dripping, dropping, dropping to the ground
As the snow turns to slush
The children have to come in
The twirling snow has disappeared.

Sarah Milne (10)
Bentley Heath Primary School

Cauldrons

Eye of reptile, skin of snake,
Stir it round with a rusty old rake.
Tail of cat, fangs from bat,
Put it all in a 5 litre vat.
Add some salt and pepper too,
Don't worry, it's a witches' brew.

Foot of frog, leg of dog,
Then dump it in a big old log.
Put in a hat, an ear from a rat,
Then dump it on a big old mat.

Anna McNeillie (9)
Bentley Heath Primary School

The Story Of Red Riding Hood Continued . . .

Red Riding Hood had soon grown up,
No longer did she drink from her baby cup.
Now she was married
And now she carried,
A girl with a golden curl.

This special girl with a golden curl,
Was as precious as a glistening pearl,
She had two teeth,
Beneath her rosy cheeks
And was named Purple Riding Hood.

Purple Riding Hood set out one day,
As she was going far away,
She took a basket full of cakes,
That her mother had finally baked
And off she went to the woods.

To the woods she had went,
Through the trees which had been bent,
Over the hills
And through the mills,
Over to Great Granny's house.

There in Granny's bed sat a large pinky head,
It had two round eyes
And chubby thighs
And it leapt on Purple Hood's feet.

'Ow!' she screamed as she fell,
'I think I've fallen over a bell!'
Her father heard the bell ring,
So he rushed to the pinky thing,
Great Granny then took her knife
And killed the thing with all her might.

Sheniz Shefik (10)
Bentley Heath Primary School

A Mysterious Beast

In the blackest night,
Far away in the woods,
There was a magnificent sight
And on a rock it stood.

With razor-sharp teeth
And horns like a devil,
It was so tall,
There was no man at his level

And with horrible eyes,
With a horrible glare,
Nobody in the world,
Could look at his stare.

It moved through the dark,
Like a night-time shadow
And had spikes on its back,
Those were as green as a meadow.

On its gigantic body,
It had some massive wings
And when it did bite,
It caused a painful sting.

But it did not like the Earth,
So it flew to the heavens,
Where it shall rest in peace,
Forever and ever.

Shankho Chaudhuri (10)
Bentley Heath Primary School

Stripe

Dark black stripes,
Upon the glistening body,
Lying beside his dying mother,
Sorrowful eyes watching her fade away,
His caring father hunting to keep them alive.

His father beckons him to go to bed,
But he can't sleep because he longs for his mother,
But his mother's dead
And gone forever.

Lauren Pindar (9)
Bentley Heath Primary School

Summery Sun

When I go out in the sun,
It melts my ice cream,
My mum says put on sun lotion,
So I don't get burnt.

In the summer when it's sunny
I sweat so bad,
It feels like I've got loads of clothes on,
Even with my glasses on it's blinding.

Sometimes I get
Out the paddling pool
The heat is so bad
So that means I've got to go in now.

Casey Fox (7)
Blackwood School

Hullabaloo At Wet Play

There's hullabaloo in the classroom,
There's hullabaloo in the hall,
There's hullabaloo in the dining room,
There's no peace at all.

The whistle is blown,
This means wet play,
The children come in,
Hip, hip, hooray.

It's five-past one,
Suddenly there's an almighty twang,
The children pack away,
Because the bell has rang.

Thomas Wait (9)
Blackwood School

The Fox

His eyes flashing like lightning as he passed through the woods,
His snout wet as a damp leaf,
His ears pricked up at any sign of movement,
His blood-red coat soft as silk can be,
His bushy sunset tail swished side to side as he walked,
His sharp and sparkling teeth
Waiting to taste his prey's flesh,
His tummy lurching with excitement
And rumbling like a volcano.

Fiona Spencer (8)
Blackwood School

The Giggles

When I get the giggles,
They never seem to stop.
I always start to wiggle,
Until I burst or pop.

It starts off in my tummy
And enters to my head,
When I think of something funny,
I can never go to bed.

I have them in the school line,
They last right up till break,
I have them again at dinner time,
I cannot concentrate.

So when you start to giggle,
Please take note of this . . .
Giggles are not funny,
When you're a teacher, Miss!

Annie Walker (9)
Blackwood School

Hungry Foxes

Hungry foxes at night,
Eyes shining bright.
Looking in bins for food,
In a happy sneaky mood.
Avoiding buses and cars,
Making his way home under the stars.
His fur bright red, tail all bushy,
Collecting leaves to make his bed cushy.
Twitchy whiskers, springy legs,
Being nosy in people's sheds.
Crafty smile and big fat belly,
Sniffing at a thrown-away welly.

Isaac Shepherd (7)
Blackwood School

Shady Garden Grow

Shady garden grow,
Where red flowers blow,
Trees glistening in the garden snow,
We pray for this to happen,
Shady garden grows.

Shady garden grow,
Here comes the sun,
Let's have some fun,
We pray for this to happen,
Shady garden grows.

Shady garden grow,
Can we have some snow?
See the treetops covered
In a white magical carpet,
We pray for this to happen,
Shady garden grows.

Shady garden grow,
Listen to the birds' song,
Hearing the fountain splash and flow,
This season lasts for long,
We pray for this to happen,
Shady garden grows.

Sabrina Chamba (8)
Blackwood School

The Garden Fox

Night-time sees the fox awake,
From the man's garden the food he will take,
His tummy is rumbling,
His bright eyes glow,
The crafty fox will not be slow.

Victoria Maher (8)
Blackwood School

The Rain

The rain
Roars down onto the ground

The rain
Pours down onto us

The rain
Thrashes down onto houses

The rain
Hammers down onto the trees

The rain
Pounds down onto some animals

The rain
Drops down into the rivers

The rain
Falls down to form puddles.

Oliver Peake (7)
Blackwood School

The Sun

In the summer the sun shines
Like a burning fire
In the summer the sun melts you
Like an ice cream melting
In the summer the sun dazzles you
Like a blind person
In the summer the pond glitters
Like you're about to cry
In the summer you're burning
Like a radiator that's on full blast.

Monique Sall (7)
Blackwood School

It's Snowing Today!

It's snowing today
As I go out to play
The pavements are glistening
The postman is whistling
As he tries to stay on his feet
The traffic is slow
There's no way to go
Until the sun shines down with some heat

The birds they are chirping
Up in the trees they are lurking
Wondering what to eat
Their foodstuff is gone
So we must help them along
And give them our scraps as a treat

The gardens are all white
It must have fallen through the night
So silent it came, this frozen rain
Looking like a carpet of fluff
All this cold wet stuff
It's snow, it's snow, it's snow!

Emma Lowe (9)
Blackwood School

There Is Something In The Sea

There is something in the sea
I think it begins with D
It's a big creature and it goes deeper and deeper
I wonder what it could be?
Splash! Splash! Splash!
I know, it's a dolphin
That splashes around all day
I wonder what a dolphin is thinking right now
As it splashes happily through the waves?

Tyra Robinson (7)
Blackwood School

My Brother Is . . .

My brother is boring,
He's rude to me,
He likes to be silly,
Especially in front of me,
He loves to fight with me,
But sometimes things go wrong
And I go off crying,
Singing a sad song.

Rachel Davis (8)
Blackwood School

The Thunderstorm

Thunder! Thunder!
Whacking the earth!
Lightning! Lightning!
Zooming around!
Hear the hail crashing to the ground
And the thunder quaking the earth.
The rain is still heavy,
The sky and clouds are black and grey,
What a nasty storm this is today . . .

Adam Carrington (8)
Blackwood School

Animals

A is for ape who can swing very far
N is for newt who can run very fast
I is for insects small, thin and sneaky
M is for monkey with a very long tail
A is for antelope with sharp, pointed horns
L is for lion with his mighty roar
S is for snake who slips and slides around.

Alice Keen (8)
Blackwood School

Sweet Shop

I walked into a sweet shop
What did I see?
Lots of sweets
Hopefully for me!
Chocolates on the shelf,
Gums on the desk,
Sweets are the best
And the shopkeeper thinks I'm a pest.
I walk back home on my own,
Although I still moan.

Georgia Cash (10)
Blackwood School

My Family

F is for family, that's me, Mum and Jay
A is for arguments, that's me and Jay but we call it play
M is for Mum, the boss of the house
I is for Izzy, that's my pet mouse
L is for lie 'cause I don't have a mouse, I just wrote that
because it rhymed with house!
Y is for yellow, the colour of the sun, you've just met my family,
that's me, Jay and Mum.

Thomas Duggan (7)
Blackwood School

Chocolate

I love chocolate
It's plain to see
I love chocolate
It's yummy, yummy, yummy.

There's dark, white and milk chocolate, my favourite
It tastes lovely
And that's why I love it!

Jade Slater (9)
Blackwood School

Our School

Our school is the best,
Maths, English and the rest.

They do teach us very well,
But we love it when they ring the bell.

We do like seeing our friends,
But we all like the weekends.

Our school is really cool
And that's why it's called . . .

Blackwood School!

Megan Phillips (9)
Blackwood School

The Very Nasty Fox

The fox in the street is a very nasty beast,
He comes around with a frightening sound,
If you see him during the night,
He might give you a terrible fright,
His ears prick up and he looks for deers,
'Here is my tea,' he cheers.

Abbie Bates (7)
Blackwood School

Wintry Weather

Nose as cold as chips in the freezer,
Toes colder than dips in the river,
No cold ice creams for the winter,
If you eat them they make you shiver,
Just eat hot soup for dinner,
Then you'll be warm all over!

Lydia Elliott-Johnson (8)
Blackwood School

The Rings

Three rings for the three great kings under the blue sky
Seven for the greedy dwarf lords in their dusty halls of stone
Nine for brave, mortal men, doomed to die
Courageous is the warrior Aragorn, heir to the throne
In the land of Mordor lives Sauron's eye
Watching over you, whether you live or die
The Orcs that are called the Uruk-hai
Are the gruesome ones with big demonic eyes
The one that bares the evil ring
To the evil king the body they will bring.

Anisha Doug (8)
Blackwood School

A Foxy Fable

In the middle of the night
When the stars twinkle bright
There is a fox who is looking for food
When he is hungry, he is always in a very bad mood
His eyes are as yellow as the sun
His nose is as shiny as a silver coin
His tail is as bushy as a brush
His fur is as sleek as silk.

Emily Egan (7)
Blackwood School

Burning Sun

The sun is burning in your face
It's roasting your legs till they turn into ash
Your arms are sweating like the rain
Your toes are flaming like the sun
Your hands are boiling with warmth in them
And your neck has blinding heat
And your back is shining like the sun.

Robert Pol (8)
Blackwood School

Mr Fox

My sharp teeth
Can rip some beef
My pointed ears
Can hear some deer
When I run around
My plump belly almost drops to the ground
My eyes so bright
So I can see when there is no light
My bushy tail is sometimes a prize
Just look at its size!
In danger I am
Catch me if you can.

Sarah Webb (7)
Blackwood School

Wintry Weather

Great! White snow falling from the sky
It's so cold that it freezes my tie
Snowball fights make a shiver down my spine
I think snow is divine
I make my dog pull my sledge like a husky,
Now the wind is getting really gusty
I walk to school because of the road
Far too dangerous I was told
After dinner it's time for bed
'You can play tomorrow,' Mum said.

Cian Dalton (8)
Blackwood School

The Sun

The sun shines
As if it's mine

The sun's shimmering rays
Have nothing to pay

The sun is gentle
But not mental

The sun is hot
But not like a pot

The sun is roasting
And I'm not boasting.

Rebecca Croton (7)
Blackwood School

Thunder Strike

Crash!
The thunder strikes
Flash!
The thunder makes a noise
Bang!
The thunder clashes
Strike!
The thunder bangs.

Ngoh-hun Lam (8)
Blackwood School

The Flower Girls

Whenever I meet the flower girls,
They each have a flower,
You must be careful,
They've got a lot of power.

Zooming around,
As bright as light,
Whether in combat,
But boy can they fight.

There's Bluey, Pinkey, Yellow and Lilac,
There are only four,
But they make you believe,
There are many more.

When in need,
Just call the name
And things
Will never be the same.

They will help you at night
And in the day,
They do anything you want,
You just have to say.

Kelsey Chand (9)
Blackwood School

The Bright Sun

The sun is hot
The sun is bright
The sun makes you boiling hot
It comes and goes
And twinkles your nose
And makes your back very brown.

Ryan Keyte (7)
Blackwood School

The Fox's Prey

As evening descends
And the moon comes out
The fox wakes up
And creeps about
He is hungry
And in the mood
To creep around
And find some food
Into the dark and eerie woods
He's sneaking around
Listening for sound
Imagining what could be found . . .
A rustling sound is what he hears
He also sees a fluffy tail
Rabbit, rabbit, a meal, he thinks
That should be tasty, where's the drinks?

Jamie Walker (8)
Blackwood School

Fox

My eyes gleam like the sun,
My legs go like lightning,
My nose twitches like a mouse,
My ears prick up when I hear my prey,
My mouth drips with saliva,
My white teeth glow in the dark,
The ground crunches as I step on twigs,
I am camouflaged in my surroundings.

Liam Wallbank (8)
Blackwood School

The Fox In The Box

The fox in the box
Was angry
The fox in the box
Was mad
The fox was hungry
He was sad
His smooth fur was starting
To darken
He rolled and rolled
Until he was free
Being free, it was glee
It was heaven!
He sprinted and pounced
And smiled and bounced
He chased a mouse
Around his house
Out in a field
He found his own family
They lived together
Forever very happily.

Joseph Davies (8)
Blackwood School

Foxy Poem

Mr Fox runs
As fast as he can
Running after his dinner

His eyes are as bright
As the stars

His coat is as
Bright as the sun

You better watch out
Because he'll pounce on you.

Stacie Googan (7)
Blackwood School

The Day It Snowed

I opened the curtains
And could not believe my eyes.
Snow was falling from the sky
All over the garden gleaming white,
It had snowed all through the night.

I can see a little squirrel,
He must be cold,
But he doesn't seem to mind,
He is jumping and skipping around
Then digging holes in the snow
To see what food he can find.

As I watch from my window,
The snowflakes look just like little stars,
And then disappear when they land
On the top of the cars.

Now I must get dressed quickly,
To go outside and play.
I want to build a snowman,
Before all that snow just melts away!

Andrew Barnes (9)
Blanford Mere Primary School

Wind

He swiftly and sharply whipped around the trees,
Howling like a wolf but softly crying,
He grabbed the sun
And locked it away in a dark and cloudy dungeon,
His heartbeat sounds like thunder,
Though it is very, very heavy and strong!

Sharnie Whitehouse (10)
Blanford Mere Primary School

African Drumming

Brown hands thumping the skin-like texture with soft fur,
Boom, boom, boom! says the talking drum as the crisp sun rises.
A tribal dance around the fire somersaults, *boom, boom*!
goes the djembe,
The stars are twinkling in the ink-like sky, *ca, ca!* cries out
the goblet drum.

Groovy rhythms going through your head,
Learning about djembes, goblet drums, talking drums
and much more.
The African sun scorching down on the plain, *doom, doom!*
goes the djembe again,
Giraffes raise their thin, slender heads towards the sun.

Hollow wood pine in a barrel shape with skin on each end,
Wrinkled hands hit each, making beautiful music.
The grass moves and sways to the music,
The grass is like a half verdant and half brown sea.

So ends my poem but there are more things I could say,
When you have a drum placed in your grasp your heart fills with glee!
It is like your hands are super-glued to the drum,
The rhythms keep growing like a huge oak tree.

Laura Evans (10)
Blanford Mere Primary School

The Wind

The wind is a wolf howling through cities,
The wind is like a small mouse whispering past trees,
The wind is so strong it turns umbrellas inside-out,
The wind can be as deadly as wild fire,
The wind is a strong storm
And it breaks branches off trees.

Matthew Brookes (10)
Blanford Mere Primary School

The Wind

The wind is like a ferocious beast,
Searching for its prey
And as it grows day by day,
It finds a way to play!

The wind is like a soft hooting owl,
Searching for its worms
And as it makes us squirm and squirm,
It thinks, *hey, they're only worms!*

The wind is like a hovering bird,
Searching for a field mouse
And once he has found that little mouse,
He goes and perches on the top of a house!

The wind is like a sleeping hamster,
Searching for a dream,
Then it suddenly comes to him,
He's not supposed to dream.

Amy Wright (10)
Blanford Mere Primary School

What Will It Taste Like?

A cup of love to make Christmas warm,
A packet of fun to make it jolly,
A jug full of happiness to make it happy,
A spoonful of laughter to make it cheerful,
Stir it with peace to make it a calm time,
Bake it with care to make it just right,
Serve it with smiles to make it special.

Bethany Fisher (10)
Blanford Mere Primary School

At Dudley Town Hall

We went to a concert
At Dudley Town Hall
Our whole class went
There was room for us all

We went to play drums
We'd been taught in our school
By Jorj, Lisa and Pat of 'Drumlove'
We thought they were *cool!*

We were very excited
As we started to play
The audience clapped loudly
They made our day

African was my favourite
But I liked Bangra as well
Steel drum and dancing
The whole thing was *swell!*

Anna Holyoake (10)
Blanford Mere Primary School

The Wind

Gentle wind slow and mild,
It seems to be more tame than wild.

The blusters of the wind leaves falls,
It seems like butterflies galore.

Stronger, stronger, branches crack,
Like an angry animal's snap.

The wind sounds like wolves howling,
The trees bend as if they're cowering.

The wind dies down until there seems
No sound and birds come out to sing.

Nicola Barlow (11)
Blanford Mere Primary School

History Is So Cool!

History is so cool,
Even though it's at school,
The court jesters are jiving,
Sir Henry Ford is driving,
That's why it's so cool.

History is so cool,
Even though it's at school,
The hippies are in the fields,
The Romans have got their shields,
That's why it's so cool.

History is so cool,
Even though it's at school,
The pirates are killing,
The Aztecs are thrilling,
That's why it's so cool.

History is so cool,
Even though it's at school,
Guy Fawkes was so mean,
The Tudors aren't at all clean,
That's why it's so cool.

Sophie Burchell (10)
Blanford Mere Primary School

A Recipe For Christmas

A cup of joy for a girl and boy,
A packet of snow to make it glow,
A jug full of light to make it bright,
A spoonful of glee to make it happy,
Stir it with a smile,
Bake it in the oven with glee,
Serve it to the family and me.

Ben Edwards (10)
Blanford Mere Primary School

Henry VIII

Young Henry with his golden hair
His complexion was delicate and fair
What a handsome man he was
Tall and broad with blue eyes

How he loved to spend his money
On fancy clothes with lots of jewels
Off to France to fight some wars
Henry made a lot of laws

Henry VIII was often wedded
Two of his wives were beheaded!
His true love was Queen Jane
Who lost her life bearing a male child

Then what became of poor Henry
Too much drinking, too much eating
No longer handsome and admired
Now bad-tempered, fat and tired.

Scarlett Yates (8)
Blanford Mere Primary School

African Drumming

Drumlove are good at playing the drums,
I thought it was good,
Lots of people came to watch, even my mum,
The drums were made of wood,
Drumlove came into school,
Their names were Lisa, Jorj and Pat,
I thought they were really cool,
There was a special drum,
It needed a mat!

Ruby Davies (9)
Blanford Mere Primary School

Art

Art, art, I love art, to do art you don't have to be smart,
In art you can draw almost anything, such as a horse and cart.

I love art because you can colour in all types of ways such as:
Felt pens and paints, you can even do it with your mates.

Paints are brilliant, paints are fun, if you do it really well
You could even impress your mum.

With papier-mâché you can do much more
The paper and glue allow you to explore.

Pens are tools we use to write,
But you can use them to make the drawing look right.

We use glue to stick things together
And sometimes, they can be together forever.

James Jevons (9)
Blanford Mere Primary School

The Lead Seagull On His Throne

The lead seagull likes to be known,
As being bossy and sitting on his throne,
His throne is high, as a high oak tree,
The school building is where he likes to be,
His voice cackles through the street,
Hearts trembling as people meet,
Him sitting high, proud and tall,
'I am the boss' he likes to call,
'If you come close I will shout
Get off my land! Get off! Get out!'
Birds will fly and leave him alone,
On his precious, royal throne.

Georgia Davis (11)
Blanford Mere Primary School

Snow

Blankets of white cover the ground,
Crunching footsteps all around.
Children hurtle down the hill,
Mothers watch from the window sill.

No flowers seen just lots of snow,
A frost tree, a freezing breeze.
No school today,
Hooray!

Charlotte Richards (9)
Blanford Mere Primary School

Snow Is . . .

Snow is calm
Snow is white
Snow is falling
All through the night!

Snow is fluffy
Snow is fun
But soon is melted
By the sun!

Megan Burda (9)
Blanford Mere Primary School

Rain

He is like a heartbeat thumping
And reaching out in horror,
The rain is stomping down the stairs,
Like some drums banging in fear.

Shaun Palmer (10)
Blanford Mere Primary School

Snow

Snowflakes fall, snowflakes glide,
All the way down from the night sky.

Snow glistens on the ground,
As it has fallen all around.

Children play with the snow,
They make tracks as they go.

As the sun comes out,
The snow begins to melt.

Grace Massey (9)
Blanford Mere Primary School

A Recipe For Christmas

A cup of fun to make Christmas special,
A packet of presents to make it giving,
A jug full of snow to make it white,
A spoonful of Santa to make it magic,
Bake it in the oven for Jesus,
Serve it to family because what would Christmas be without them!

Helena Forrest (11)
Blanford Mere Primary School

Rain

The sound of his heartbeat drumming the ground
Sharply and swiftly whipping round the trees
The screeching screams and loud cries of a vain sound
Powerful raindrops falling over mountains and seas
With roars and bangs raging with fear
Each raindrop's like a glittering tear.

Charlotte Gordon (11)
Blanford Mere Primary School

A Recipe For Christmas . . .

A cup of fun to make Christmas special,
A cup of peace for all to share,
A jug of happiness to bring it all near,
A spoonful of laughter to make a cheer,
Stir it and make a wish for this day,
Bake for hope
And serve to make Christmas easy to cope!

Heather Proudler (10)
Blanford Mere Primary School

The Wind

The wind blows on a cold dark night,
Howling like a lonely wolf,
The wind gets louder and louder,
Cutting through the trees above,
Animals and birds hide away,
Scared that the wind may not go away,
But slowly and surely, the wind
Does stray away, away, away.

Emily Cresswell (11)
Blanford Mere Primary School

The Wind

The wind is like a howling dog
Rummaging through the freezing fog
As it rumbles to and fro
Loosening all the glistening snow

As it whistles with the sun
Lots of people having fun
When they discover the wind appear
They start to dash and tremble with fear.

Patrick James (10)
Blanford Mere Primary School

The Wind

Blowing at the trees
Whispering through the leaves
Howling, crashing through fences knocking things down
Whooshing through the town
Blowing hard as can be blown
Never blowing high or low
Just wondering where next to go
Slowing down, getting worn out
Quietening down, never intending to shout
Calming down and falling to sleep.

Laura Fellows (11)
Blanford Mere Primary School

PE Time

Running, jumping, skipping, hopping,
Full of energy,
It's fun being part of a team,
Who will win?

Dancing, leaping, throwing, catching,
Keeping fit,
Following the rhythm,
At PE time.

Claire Poultney (9)
Blanford Mere Primary School

June

There once was a girl called June
Who said she could play a tune
She said, 'Listen to me
Hang on, I've pressed the wrong key'
She could do it for her honeymoon.

Stuart Brown (11)
Blanford Mere Primary School

Snow

I love to see the soft white snow,
Falling to the ground,
I love to see the snowflakes,
That settle all around.

I look out of the window
To see a blanket of white,
No footprints or anything to see,
Oh! What a beautiful sight.

I go out to play in the snow,
With my best friend, Jane,
The clouds are grey in the sky,
Oh no! It's started to rain.

Samantha Oakley (9)
Blanford Mere Primary School

A Christmas Recipe!

A cup of happiness to make Christmas cheerful,
A pocket of peace to make it joyful,
A jug of kindness to make it unforgettable,
A spoonful of generosity to make it special.
Stir it with a Christmas wish to make your dreams come true,
Bake it with magic to give a touch of Christmas spirit,
Serve it with an abundance of love to give everyone a time to enjoy!

Laura Pike (11)
Blanford Mere Primary School

Rain

The rain pouring like a leopard hunting
And a row of drums all beating,
He growls fiercely like a raging tiger,
Then finally it shatters into a thousand pieces
When it touches the ground.

Allanah Hickman (11)
Blanford Mere Primary School

Art

Art is fun,
It's really great.
Third lesson Tuesday,
I can't wait.

Colours and textures,
Everywhere,
Junk modelling or drawing,
I don't care.

Painting, shading,
Mark making too.
Charcoal and sketching
And sticking with glue.

I do art at home
And art at school,
As you can see,
It's really cool.

Victoria Mason (9)
Blanford Mere Primary School

Snow, Snow

Snow, snow how do you fall?
Like a diamond on the floor.

Snow, snow how do you crunch?
Like someone going munch, munch, munch.

Snow, snow how do you freeze?
Like an ice cube in the night breeze.

Snow, snow how do you melt?
Very quickly with the warmth felt.

Luke Stevens (8)
Blanford Mere Primary School

A Gust Of Wind

The wind is howling like a big fierce wolf
Through the forest,
I look at the flowers blowing in the wind,
They remind me of a nearby florist.
The wind sounds like it is whispering,
Like a quiet heron searching for fish in a river.
The wind is like a flickering moth by a fire
With a shiver.
The wind blows fast and hard, down the street,
Blowing people's umbrellas inside-out.
The wind is like a whale blowing air out of his blowhole,
The wind blows the leaves up and about,
The wind is like a huge bear breaking the branches off the trees,
People struggle to keep on their feet
But end up on their knees!

Katrina Hughes (10)
Blanford Mere Primary School

Snow Is Falling

Snow is falling, what a day,
As I rush out on my sleigh,
Children going down the hill,
Hitting snowmen standing still.

Snowballs flying here and there,
Frozen fingers, we don't care,
Walking, slipping, falling down,
All this happens in the town.

The snow is melting, I've had a good day,
Water is running all the way,
Down the hill the water flows,
Gulped by the drains and away it goes.

Rhys Williams (9)
Blanford Mere Primary School

The Wind

The wind is like a polar bear,
Whispering, whispering through the air,
As cold as it could ever be,
Let me warm myself up with a cup of tea.

The wind could be warm on a sunny day,
Like a kangaroo, in the desert in May,
Keep me cool with the summer breeze,
I like hot and cold, can I have warm please?

The wind can be warm, also cold and hot,
Like a little warm ant you could catch in a pot,
I like it hot with a little summer's breeze,
I like it cold, but I don't want to freeze.

The wind has a life just like you and me,
One that no one can ever see,
The wind could blow at your knees,
The wind always blows straight at me.

Sarah Whitehouse (11)
Blanford Mere Primary School

A Recipe For All The World

A cup of love for all the world,
A packet of peace for all to share,
A jug of water for those who need it most,
A spoonful of happiness to bring cheerful faces.

Stir it to make hope,
Bake it for a few hours
And serve it to hungry people
To bring Christmas joy.

Lucy Giacomin (10)
Blanford Mere Primary School

The Wind

The wind blows gently through the trees,
Like dancing and prancing honeybees,
It keeps the day lovely and cool,
Like a penguin waddling through his pool,
But it changes to a stronger breeze.

The wind howls like a hungry bear,
Making the night have a cold chill in the air,
Breaking branches off a tree
And waiting for its mystery,
To make you *stop, look and stare!*

The wind gets rough as it storms through the sea,
As it emerges up to the top fiercely,
It comes out the sea with a mighty *roar*,
Like an African elephant banging down a door,
The wind, how I like the changes
Or is that just me?

Amy Lane (10)
Blanford Mere Primary School

Snow

The snow is blank it is a sheet
Without it the world would be incomplete
It camouflages many things
Like polar bears and the dove
But it brings great trouble to countries
Like Scotland and high above
Loads of children are glad
Because their schools are going to close
Until they realise
That their toes are froze!

Emma Watson (9)
Blanford Mere Primary School

School Rap!

I really like school
It's fab and it's cool
The teachers aren't boring
We don't sleep or start snoring
But I wish the teachers would nap
So I could secretly rap
Art is great
I draw and paint on slate!

I really like school
It's fab and it's cool
D and T's not hard
Because we make things out of card
Maths is fun
When you know the answer to the sum
We learn things in history
And science we solve the mystery!

I really like school
It's fab and it's cool
If your handwriting's neat at the age of 10
You can use an ink pen
PE, we have exercise and fun
We do netball, dance and run
We should all like school
Because it's fab and it's cool!

Amy Cresswell (9)
Blanford Mere Primary School

Villa Vs Bolton

Villa thought they were going to win
But Bolton scored five to nil
So far Bolton in the lead
Villa then made them bleed
Villa scored a cracking goal
Then goalkeeper began to roll
Then they went on to win.

Alex Willetts (10)
Colley Lane Primary School

Once Upon A Rhyme

I put on my helmet and drift
Prowling round like a lost cat
Mysteries of the Milky Way
Along my dusty path
The rocky wasteland which at a touch
Crumbles into the atmosphere
Over the desolate land that breaks at my feet
Look! A glowing orange flower
That flower is the sun
Does that crater enclose a hideous life form
Waiting to descend upon my soul?
Although I wonder, I must return home -
Too soon I get summoned back to report my findings
I wish to stay since it's so silent
But I must return to the dreadfully noisy Earth.

Rachael Cullen (10)
Colley Lane Primary School

Holiday

Holidays are the best
Holidays are for rest
So never be a pest

Ice cream is less
Candy is a mess
But never make a guess

Children in the pool
Mums and dads are fools
Everyone shakes and gets their tools.

Intesar Lashram (8)
Colley Lane Primary School

The Magic Box

(Based on 'Magic Box' by Kit Wright)

I will position in my box . . .
The sound of a cunning cat catching a crow,
The crunch of a snake crawling through autumn leaves fallen,
A smell of a cup of coffee just poured.

I will position in my box . . .
The hottest furnace and the coldest iceberg,
The aroma of a roast dinner with gravy,
The sight of a sunset in an orange sky.

I will position in my box . . .
An eighth sea and a fifth ocean,
A jockey driving a car
And a motorist on a horse.

My box is assembled from
An old oak, leaves and a bear's coat,
With ancient forests on the lid and forgotten tales in the corners
And mechanical inventions never seen as hinges.

I will explore in my box of past, present and future,
Till the time has come then drift off to a
Faraway paradise island.

Daniel Parsons (9)
Colley Lane Primary School

Sophie

Sophie told the worst excuses
When she was asked to do something, she fuses
The worst excuse that she has told so far
Is her need for a car
Her mum asked, 'Why?'
'So I can be a spy'
She tries her hardest to give her reason
During every single season
With no luck, she gives up
And asks her mum for a pup!

Stacie Hingley (10)
Colley Lane Primary School

The Magic Box

(Based on 'Magic Box' by Kit Wright)

I will place in my box . . .
The scent of a fresh summer morning,
The heat from the blazing hot sun,
The whoosh of the wind on a winter's night,

I will place in the box . . .
The sound of the Devil,
The greasy hair of a witch from the past,
The first smile of a newborn

I will place in my box . . .
A sun without any shine,
Water that changes colour
And a fish that swims on dry land.

My box will be designed with ice,
Water and rubies,
With elephants on the lid and mysteries in the corners,
Its hinges from a mermaid's scale far across the sea.

I shall sing a lullaby in my box
To a baby oh, so fine,
Then bring it back home,
Out of my fabulous dream.

Abigail Ward (9)
Colley Lane Primary School

My Sister

My sister is a little girl
She often likes to give a twirl
She can be good or sometimes bad
She sometimes goes to hug my dad
My sister likes to play and sing
So she messes with all my things
But I love her lots and lots
Then she ties me up in knots.

Shaun Haywood (10)
Colley Lane Primary School

School Is The Best

School is the best
Never mind the rest
Just beat the quest
Turn to the west
Don't be a pest

Fizz, fizz, whizz, whizz
Turn your hair like this
Please and thank you
All to the rest
You'll be impressed

Work is the best
Give it a rest
Wait for the test
So school is the best.

Naseera Lashram (10)
Colley Lane Primary School

David Beckham

David Beckham trains very hard,
David Beckham's got a red card,
David's mate is called Ryan Giggs,
David's got two little kids,
David's got loads of cash,
David's normally very flash.
'I'm afraid David's playing football,
I'll get him to give you a call.'

Daniel Whitehouse (10)
Colley Lane Primary School

The Magic Box

(Based on 'Magic Box' by Kit Wright)

I will place in my box . . .
The mayor's man-made medal,
The Indian shout of life
And the mist of the seven seas

I will place in my box . . .
A bite of the whitest cloud on Earth
The biggest scarecrow in England
And the soul of a puppy

I will place in my box . . .
The thirteenth month and the eighth day
An invisible pencil
And yellow transparent air

My box is constructed by the sun
Ice and the lava of the biggest volcano
It's got diamonds on the lid, ancient symbols in the corners
Its hinges are the troll's giant foot

I will hover in my box and spawn wings
Then enchant time so I can change the past
And change my dreams and have a better future.

Adam Bunn (10)
Colley Lane Primary School

Winter

He covers the land in a white sheet of frost,
But comes greatly at Mother Nature's cost.
He strips the trees bare,
He makes the children stare
At the snow outside.
He covers the land in a white sheet of frost,
But comes greatly at Mother Nature's cost.

Sam Fowkes (11)
Colley Lane Primary School

The Magic Box

(Based on 'Magic Box' by Kit Wright)

I will lie in my box . . .
The fin from the bluest whale swaying his tail,
A flame from the furious furnace,
A golden halo from around an angel's head.

I will lie in my box . . .
The earliest cry of a baby in need of help,
The pattern from a snake sliding through the sand,
New skin from a delicate baby.

I will lie in my box . . .
A white sun and red-hot rain,
A baby with the skin of a witch,
A dog with a halo of an angel.

My box is decorated from sand, fire and water,
With plants on the lid and tales in the corners,
Its hinges are the teeth from a mighty lion.

I shall drift in my box
And hear tales of an ancient uncle
And surf away to a long-lost island
In the middle of the sea.

Liam Massey (10)
Colley Lane Primary School

My Dog

My dog sometimes is a pest,
But he tries his best,
He likes long walks,
He never talks,
My dog is black and white and brown,
He likes to go to the town,
He adores you tickling his belly,
But best of all is watching telly.

Jemma Greaves (10)
Colley Lane Primary School

The Snow/The Sour Lemon

The Snow
The snow on the windows looks
Shiny
Sparkling
It's special
Silver

The Sour Lemon
The lemon on my tongue tastes
Sugary
Sour
It's special
Sweet.

Stacy Silvers (10)
Colley Lane Primary School

The Lady Of Shalott

(Based on 'The Lady Of Shalott by Alfred Lord Tennyson)

We should take our time
To see this crime
Her lips like wine
Her dress like lime
In many towered Camelot
He clenched his fist
They were in the mist
She will always exist
The Lady of Shalott.

Luke Hadley (9)
Colley Lane Primary School

The Lady Of Shalott

(Based on 'The Lady of Shalott' by Alfred Lord Tennyson)

Who could do this terrible deed?
For this woman is in need
I shall take her on my steed
And I shall ride with all my speed
All the way to Camelot
Who has done this awful crime?
For we are wasting important time
Now she will always be mine
The Lady of Shalott.

James Taylor (9)
Colley Lane Primary School

Lady Of Shalott

(Based on 'The Lady of Shalott' by Alfred Lord Tennyson)

He felt sad as he stood near
Thee who stands now all must hear
'I shall never live in fear
I will never cry a tear
In many towered Camelot
I shall love with all my heart
We will never be apart'
Placed her into my cart
The Lady of Shalott.

Derrie Pearson (10)
Colley Lane Primary School

Smelly Nelly

There was a young lady named Nelly,
Who was so awfully smelly,
She lived in a house,
With her pet mouse,
She has an enormous belly.

She sits on the sofa in front of the telly,
Eating a big bowl of ice cream and jelly,
She eats so much,
She can't even touch
Her toes because of her belly.

Katie Williams (9)
Colley Lane Primary School

Snow

The snow in the sky looks
Gentle
Gritty
It's gleaming
Glacial

The snow in the sky feels
Soft
Slushy
It's silky
Slick.

Mitchel Collins (10)
Colley Lane Primary School

Ten Little Schoolboys

(Based on 'Ten Little Children' by A A Milne)

Once upon a rhyme,
Ten little schoolboys said the weather was fine,
One went out and got frizzled up, then there were nine.

Nine little schoolboys were at the market buying bait,
A shark came and ate one, then there were eight.

Eight little schoolboys looking up at Heaven,
One went in an aeroplane, then there were seven.

Seven little schoolboys were at karate doing kicks,
One said, 'I've had enough of this!' Then there were six.

Six little schoolboys learning how to dive,
One turned into a porpoise, then there were five.

Five little schoolboys went to see a boar,
He kicked one out of the farm, then there were four.

Four little schoolboys hiding in a tree,
One got stuck in it, then there were three.

Three little schoolboys were in a cinema going 'Boo!'
Someone booted one out, then there were two.

Two little schoolboys went out to Wilkinson,
One got lost in there, then there was one.

One little schoolboy, a chair he sat upon,
He fell off, down a hole, then there were *none!*

Richard Raithby (7)
Colley Lane Primary School

The Tiger

Eyes of beady rubies
Fur like soft swaying silk
Teeth like sharp razors
As he stalks the land.

Amy Dyer (8)
Greswold Primary School

The Kitten

As he curls up soft and small,
Playing with his favourite yellow ball,
While everything compared to him is so tall.

As she lies silently under a table,
With a Christmas tree and a tiny straw stable,
To move without being heard she is able.

Isabella Shore (8)
Greswold Primary School

The Owl

Midnight has come, the owl is awake,
Grazing over the moonlit lake,
Getting ready to take.

Suddenly like a bolt of thunder he flashes,
He has not caught his prey but he had crashes,
Like a jet his prey thrashes.

James Daglish (8)
Greswold Primary School

The Mouse

A mouse of fur, full of dirt,
A tail as long as a snake,
His eyes like fire balls,
He scampers away into the night.

Alex Jarvis (9)
Greswold Primary School

The Tiger

His back like a smooth blanket,
His teeth like sharp, sharp knives,
There he lies with his family pack
And he strides away looking for food.

Elliesha Gill (8)
Greswold Primary School

The Mouse

A tiny creature with a tail of swirls,
Eyes like glowing spirals,
Ears are like two pointy curls,
It pounces from one end to the other
Into the dark, gloomy woods.

Paramvir Kaur Dhanda (8)
Greswold Primary School

The Waterfall

It is a glass of water,
    Being poured from a high cliff.
It is a blue piece of thread,
    Trying to put glitter on itself.
It is some light blue paint,
    Squirting from a mountaintop.
It is a plateful of blue, wobbly jelly,
    Falling into a hard mouth.
It is an ink pen leaking,
    Through some heavy stones.
It is a shiny silver tap,
    Ready to have a drink from.

Rizwana Kirun (10)
Halesowen CE Primary School

I'm Scared

I'm full of fear, I hear a tiger roaring,
I see a cheetah running from the sky,
The darkness, the fright, nothing feels right,
The rain is tapping at my windowpane,
Pitter-patter, it's cold, I shiver,
I'm still, instead of like a flowing river,
The noise!
I try to play with my toys,
My room shakes, my favourite doll breaks,
I'm full of fear,
All I hear is a scream,
I see lightning gleam,
I shiver again,
The rain knocks on my window, wanting to come in,
My heart pounds fearfully like a rhythmical drum,
My television seems fuzzy,
The light goes, whilst the wind furiously blows,
The rain slows down,
But suddenly turns into hard, hurtful hail, I grow cold.
On the weather I was told it would be like this,
I lie in bed, again the wind blows,
All the power goes, my heart is cold,
I'm full of fright, it's a cold, cold night,
A tear races down my cheek,
I'm cold, I need a hand to hold, I move the cover from my face,
Then my heart starts to race,
I open the curtains to find . . . the rain has stopped,
I feel that I wasn't at all scared,
Then I peacefully fall asleep.

Laura Heeks (10)
Halesowen CE Primary School

Wintertime

Wintertime, wintertime, cold and bare
Wintertime, wintertime, not a sound in the air
The snow like a big white sheet of silk
The colour as pure as milk

Wintertime, wintertime, Jack Frost is out
Wintertime, wintertime, look out, look out
My fingers are pink like the morning sky
I wish I could get my hands on a big hot pie

Wintertime, wintertime, the children emerge
Wintertime, wintertime, with a great urge
With their gloves, coats and scarves
And you can hear their millions of laughs.

Stephanie Cunneen (11)
Ham Dingle Primary School

What Am I?

Ear-pointer
Nose-twitcher
Whisker-tickler
Bobtail-lifter
Carrot-eater
Cabbage-nibbler
Clover-sniffer
Water-sipper
Currant-dropper
Fur-moulter
Hind leg-stander
Back paw-thumper
What am I?

Katie Jones (8)
Ham Dingle Primary School

Kennings - What Am I?

Wet nose
Strong-sniffer
Tail-wagger
Deep-digger
Sharp teeth
Fast-eater
Muddy paws
Speedy-runner
Loud-barker
Sloppy-licker
Hot breath
Stick-chaser
Floppy ears
Juicy bone
Comfy basket
In my home.
What am I?

Rebecca Cartwright (9)
Ham Dingle Primary School

Spring

S pring is a special time of year,
P erfect for lambs and chicks to appear,
R ed roses and rabbits come out too,
I n our eyes the sky shines blue,
N ew leaves grow on the trees,
G arden flowers attract the bees.

Lucy Arrowsmith (10)
Ham Dingle Primary School

Ballet

Getting ready to prepare
And then I'm like a bird gracefully moving through the air
Without a thought or even a care

I leap and jump with all my might
Suddenly there is a sparkling, twinkling light
Like a star gleaming bright

Audience chanting and cheering
Hundreds of people suddenly appearing
New faces, different people
I felt proud

It finally came to a big end
But hoping everyone had enjoyed
At least I was full of joy.

Helena Moss (11)
Ham Dingle Primary School

What Am I?

I am standing tall and straight like a soldier,
Guarding the street on which I shine.
My sensor tells me when to start work,
Long hours through the winter nights.
Wind can try to push me over, but I won't fall.
Like a tree, I have a root in the ground.
When my light stops shining I am useless,
Just a resting place for birds,
But then more people notice me.
A crane-truck will quickly arrive to make me bright again,
My welcoming white light helps travellers see their way home.
What am I?

Sam Clewes (7)
Ham Dingle Primary School

Spring Field

When I take a walk in the morning
There's a place where I always go
It's the field for it's always beautiful
In rain, in sun, in snow

But the time when it looks most lovely
Is the spring when the flowers grow
And the newborn lambs start jumping
And leaping to and fro

Their woolly coats are a glistening white
And their legs are smudged with black
And as they're jumping through the grass
Their tails fly on their back

And then I smell a nice sweet scent
It's the flower, purple and pink
Colours dancing in a sea of green
It's my favourite sight I think

I think that it's a magical place
Where hopes and dreams come true
It is my country paradise
And would be the same for you.

Louise Collins (10)
Ham Dingle Primary School

Grand Prix

You see all the cars on the grid glistening in the sun,
You can smell the oil and petrol that make them go
And you can hear their engines revving like roaring tigers.
You can taste the excitement as the crowd waits for the start,
You can feel the tension as the red lights go on, 1, 2, 3, 4, 5,
Then red lights out and it's go, go, go!
Michael Schumacher using his sixth sense to get away first.

Alex Moore (11)
Ham Dingle Primary School

The Theatre Trip

The usher takes my ticket and shows me to my seat,
It is deep blue velvet, as welcoming as a warm bath,
Noises all around me are like the bubbles rising to the surface,
Finally, a hush sweeps over the audience as the lights dim,
The drum rolls, the curtain rises and light fills my eyes
with wonderful colours.
The costumes are like a dozen rainbows dancing in the sky,
I gaze in wonder at the skilful dancers leaping across the stage,
Bang, the fairy godmother appears.
There's a smell of smoke like a dead firework on Bonfire Night,
Or is it the smell of magic?
I come down to Earth as the curtains close
And blink as if I've come out of a dream that I don't want to end.
As I rise from my seat I am Cinderella on my way to the ball.
The hustle and bustle around me is the guests waltzing in
time to the music,
The cold touch of the ice cream brings me to my senses
And I see the crowds around me are buzzing like bees
In anticipation of the feast that is yet to come.
I rush back to my seat, afraid of missing one beat,
The second half is about to begin.

Maddie Cole (10)
Ham Dingle Primary School

What Am I?

I'm a shape of glittering silver high above the chimney tops,
My bright light shines all through the pitch-black night,
I look just like a ballet dancer spinning through the air,
The cold wind blasts across my face
And makes me shiver and shake.
I'm passing by the Milky Way to meet my very best friends,
My shimmering body makes patterns that glow like fire in the sky.
What am I?

Sarah Collins (7)
Ham Dingle Primary School

My Football Match

I hear the crowd roaring,
They say some naughty words,
I can't repeat some of those,
As I am sure you would know!

I smell the sweet smell,
Of steak and kidney pie,
As the goalkeeper kicks the ball,
Through the clouds in the sky.

I taste the bitter smell
Of the addicts' smoke,
It's making me feel ill,
As my team
Race up the other end,
Goal 2-0.

Matthew Holloway (11)
Ham Dingle Primary School

Kennings

Slipper-pincher
Bone-beggar
Cat-chaser
Stick-fetcher
Blind-leader
Face-licker
Postman-biter
Lead-puller
Loud-barker
Person-walker
Ankle-nipper
Fox-hunter
What am I?

Hayley Bennett (8)
Ham Dingle Primary School

Magic Kingdom

M agical feelings welling up deep down inside
A nticipation of a daunting new ride
G lorious sunshine blazing down on my tanned body
I mages from movies coming to life before my eyes
C ries of delight from excited young children

K ingdom of childhood fantasy
I nstant smiles as they enter the park
N oses detecting the smell of popcorn
G rins light up the faces of the young and old
D rinking in the sights and sounds of a land far away
O nly Florida could smell, look and make you feel this way
M emories have come flooding back.

Hollie Jones (11)
Ham Dingle Primary School

What Am I?

I'm lord of the sky,
But sometimes I hide
Behind the clouds,
I run away from snow,
My enemy is rain
And I hate Jack Frost,
But I can beat all my enemies,
With my dazzling glare,
Though when the moon comes out,
I tend to hide again.
What am I?

Abigail Milne (8)
Ham Dingle Primary School

Butterflies

Butterflies, butterflies dancing in the sun,
Watching them fluttering, having such fun!
They smell like the flowers underneath the swaying trees
And look like some petals twirling in the breeze.
As they pass you without a sound,
You see them whirling round and round.
They feel like a feather tickling your skin
And you look down with a great big grin.
You try very hard not to giggle,
As they start to wriggle and wriggle.
They soon realise their mistake
And fly off to the beautiful landscape.

Samantha Gray (10)
Ham Dingle Primary School

My Life

The most important thing to me,
Is when I think of my family tree,
With all my brothers' and sisters' names,
All the fun and all the games.
With Pebbles the dog, jumping up and down,
Making all the neighbours frown,
Going to Nanny and Grandad's place,
Where the speed of living is at a slower pace.
When we go to bed at night,
Saying our prayers for others' plight,
Forget tomorrow it's out of sight.

Eleanor Martin (11)
Ham Dingle Primary School

Waterfall

Crashing, thudding among the rocks,
Here I am.
Alone.
The sun's rays shine upon me as I pick up speed,
It's a sheer drop.
I'm running down the mountainside,
I can't believe I'm doing this,
Nothing can stop me.
Nothing.
I can feel the cool air brushing against me
As I tumble down.
I'm flying.
I suddenly stop.
It's over.
I'm free.

Grace Hadley (10)
Ham Dingle Primary School

What Am I?

Wave crasher
People stasher
Palm trees tall
Seashells small
Sunbeds stunning
Children running
Sun hot
Ice creams - not
Clouds high
What am I?

Samantha Pardoe (8)
Ham Dingle Primary School

Sannibel Island

Once we arrived at the island, I saw a line of palm trees,
They were so still 'cause of the dying breeze,
In the far distance I saw the sky-blue sea,
The outlines of the ships looked great to me,
Far away I saw a dolphin diving to and fro,
Looking at the sea creatures down below.

I could hear the beat of the pelican's wings
And the distant sound of a bike bell's ring,
I could hear the gentle lapping of the waves upon the shore,
I thought that in this world there was nothing I liked more,
I could hear the peaceful rustling of the beautiful green trees
And the unbroken sound of the whispering breeze.

I could smell people cooking barbecued beef and fresh fish,
Oh, how I longed to eat that dish,
On our wondrous trip out to sea,
I smelt the salty air all around me,
As I walked along the harbour I smelt some bait,
Of the patient fishermen who lay in wait.

Perfect pink prawns were my choice for lunch
And I finished them off with an almighty crunch,
Fresh fried fish was my choice for tea,
They tasted fantastic and delicious to me,
For something sweet I chose ice cream,
The list of flavours read like a dream.

As I strolled along the beach the silky sand slipped between my toes
And when I felt the sea, my fingers nearly froze,
When I touched a dolphin it felt silky like a satin scarf
And the shells on the beach were spiky and sharp,
My skin was stroked by the rays of the sun
And I enjoyed the coolness when the day was done.

Adam Bright (10)
Ham Dingle Primary School

The Seal Surprise!

There I was blinking in the bright yellow sun,
Looking at the clear, swaying sea,
Waves crashing, the surf looking like white horses,
Dancing, prancing, galloping.
'Come out to swim with me!' shouted my friend,
Into the waves I ran, splish, splash.
'What's that?' I said
Looking into the water, a dusky grey figure slithered,
Soft like velvet, swam around my bare ankles.
It was a seal! A beautiful, smooth seal,
Gentle and soft like a baby's bottom brushed against your cheek.
Only after a couple of seconds . . . it went like a rocket into nowhere,
What a lovely sight that was.
Children were laughing, eating their ice creams with a smile!
There was a rumble in my tummy, so I ran
And as I ran I could taste the salty brine,
When I got ashore, I ate my moreish chocolate ice cream,
I sunk into the sunbed and fell asleep like that!
And that was my seal surprise!

Alexandra Lockhart (10)
Ham Dingle Primary School

A Kenning

Storm-maker
Desert-baker
Sadness-taker
Place-creator
World-lover
Huge and bigger
Super-renewer
He is greater
Who am I?

Sarah Lonergan (8)
Ham Dingle Primary School

The Goalie's Game

As I walk on the pitch I'm nerve-racked,
The kick-off's just a blur,
The smell of fairy powder whiffs under my nose,
I get sucked into the game like dust into a vacuum cleaner.
The whistle blows, free kick to us,
No noise except the shouts,
The popping ball pops up like popcorn popping in a pan.
The red and blue, the white and green,
Not the worst colours I've ever seen!
The ball's crossed in,
I make a dive,
I catch the ball in the air, I fly!
I land in the mud, I taste it, yuck!
I see a cloud, have I gone mad?
It is the white and green,
I pounce like a tiger,
Grab, the ball is mine.
The whistle blows, time up,
Now I play ball with my pup!

Ben Shave (10)
Ham Dingle Primary School

Kennings

Long-walker
Bone-burier
Toy-stealer
Tail-wagger
Loud-barker
Food-eater
Bone-digger
Toy-burier
What am I?

Emily Bastable (8)
Ham Dingle Primary School

A Poem About The Moon

The moon comes out at night,
Its colour is white,
It's the only light,
It shines very bright,
I once saw a cartoon
About a rabbit who went to the moon,
His name was Bugs Bunny,
He was very funny,
He had to come home,
Because he was all alone.

Lucy Carey (7)
Howley Grange Primary School

Boy Bobby Blue

This is a rhyme about a boy
His name was Bobby Blue
Every time he came to mine
He practised on me his kung fu
His kicks, his chops, his punches too
Then one day I kicked him back
And now he plays with Winnie the Pooh.

Opal Humphreys (9)
Howley Grange Primary School

Betty Boo

Betty Boo, I do like you
Always true
Never blue
Betty Boo I do love you
You sing so fine, rosy lips
Eyes of blue
Shoes that look like crystal tips.

Jodieleigh Swingler (9)
Howley Grange Primary School

My Family

My grandad is so funny,
He always makes me laugh,
He likes his boiled eggs runny
And eats them in the dark.

I really love my nan,
She's very nice to me,
She drives a big white van
And parks it by a tree.

I have a big fat brother,
He's sometimes nice to me,
He gets told off by Mother
And I go off with glee.

Sometimes they're quite strange,
Sometimes they're nice to me,
But I'm stuck with them forever
And that's my family.

Luke Rose (7)
Howley Grange Primary School

Summertime Is Coming

I really cannot wait,
relaxing in the sunshine, swinging on the gate.
Looking up into the sky, lovely different shades of blue
slowly floating by.
Jumping in the paddling pool,
trying to keep myself cool.
It really isn't working,
because I'm just daydreaming at school.
School is nearly over, my thoughts are nearly true,
summer is not quite here, I'll just have to see winter through.

Callum Charles (9)
Howley Grange Primary School

Out Of This World

When I stepped on the planet
There wasn't a flower
But when I saw the alien
He had some power

He spoke strangely
I didn't understand
He kept falling down
He never did stand

The strangest thing was
There wasn't a beehive
The alien ran on wheels
He'd not two eyes but five.

Amy Binnion (8)
Howley Grange Primary School

Sun!

Sun, sun, sun, I love the sun,
Because I have a lot of fun.

The sun comes out in the summertime,
I have a glassful of lemon and lime.

I have ice cubes in my glass
And I sit upon the green, green grass.

I normally go to the beach
And I've met a jellyfish and it was peach.

Sun, sun, sun, I love the sun!

Chloe Clews (8)
Howley Grange Primary School

Abating Animals

One day all animals will vanish away,
Then we will suffer and have to pay.

No more chicken or turkey drummers for tea,
Instead we will have cold potatoes, lumpy gravy and the odd pea.
Then we will notice and then we will see,
When inside our hearts we have to pay the fee.

One day all animals will vanish away,
Then we will suffer and have to pay.

Don't think I agree with eating animals - it is wrong,
Because I enjoy the whale song.
Killing elephants for their tusks - shall I take your tongue?
Why be so self-centred, just let animals live for long.

One day all animals will vanish away,
Then we will suffer and have to pay.

No more pets to take for walks,
No more dogs to watch over us like hawks.
No more pets to fetch the stick forks,
No more cuddles or barking talks.

One day all animals will vanish away,
Then we will suffer and have to pay.

Vadbhag Kaur Channa (11)
Jesson's CE Primary School

In Danger

Seals, fish, whales too,
They all suffer from pollution from you!

Lions, tigers, rhinos too,
They all suffer from what we do!

Elephants and birds have feelings too,
We upset them by the things we do!

Luke Butler (11)
Jesson's CE Primary School

The Leopard

The leopard,
one of God's creatures,
we see no more.

The leopard,
sprinting across the land,
we see no more.

The leopard,
feasting on its prey,
we see no more.

Leopard cubs,
fighting with each other,
we see no more.

Humans,
wearing a leopard-skinned coat,
we see now.

Gurpreet Natt (11)
Jesson's CE Primary School

The Bull

The bull,
How sinless is he?
His silky, leathery skin
And sharply pointed horns,
Killed for a laugh.

The matador,
How culpable is he?
Teasing his opponent,
Quivering his blood-coloured cape,
Knowing what's to happen,
Why is it his opponent who's to die?

Chelsey Dudfield (11)
Jesson's CE Primary School

Wolves

Wolves are silent and sly
When they watch the moon go by.

The moon makes the wolves howl,
Their fur is like a fluffy towel.

The wolves travel in a pack,
When they travel, they never look back.

The wolves hunt for prey,
Every night and every day.

The wolves have big padded paws,
On the end of them they have sharp claws.

But remember,
Wolves are silent and sly,
When they watch the moon go by.

Matthew Hassall (11)
Jesson's CE Primary School

Murder Or Sport?

Running, panting, twisting
The fox runs on,
Hoping for safety.

Barking, jumping, chasing, shooting!
The men gallop on,
Their dogs far ahead,
Gaining in on the fox.

The fox loses speed,
Bang! . . . A pain ceases
And now he sleeps . . .

Rachel Tudor (10)
Jesson's CE Primary School

The Bird

I am a bird
I fly, fly, fly
When I flatter my wings I go
High, high, high

I play on the clouds
I sing on the trees
When I walk on the ground
You run away from me

I eat the food that you leave
Even paper, crisps and sweets
When I eat it
I fall to the ground
And I am gone!

Aneesah Sagir (11)
Jesson's CE Primary School

A Notice To All Polar Bears

In the cold and windswept corners of our world lives the polar bear
You live in fear of being caught
Fur used for a human blanket
Something that comes of no use is wasted
You should be running with your friends, living with your family
We won't let you be left alone to live your life

So this notice might be taken into account
I will tell everyone I know that you are dying out
As slowly as the ice melts, but also as quickly as the humans kill you.

Cara Ledgister (11)
Jesson's CE Primary School

Pollution!

Baby bears
Struggle for life
But nobody cares
Pollution destroys them

Whales
Might have feelings
Watching all the rubbish destroy their homes
Everything we throw in rivers, bags, purses and combs

Polar bears
Watch each other
Their father and their mother
The babies don't know what it is
But we don't care, nobody cares
Pollution destroys them

Throwing rubbish
In the rivers
Affects all the babies' livers
They choke themselves on the things that you drop
Pollution

Pollution
Destroys lives
Destroys all living things
Pollution brings
Nothing but damage
Danger! Pollution destroys animals!

Jody Astley (10)
Jesson's CE Primary School

A Lion Poem

A lion is as strong as a whale
He is as fast as a shooting star
As lazy as an old man
As sly as a fox
A lion makes me look like a baby rat.

Javan Davis (10)
Jesson's CE Primary School

What Zoo Animals Do At Night!

Have you ever wondered what animals do at night?
Only read this poem because you might get a fright.

Never, ever go to the zoo at night,
There are animals everywhere,
If you don't want to get a fright,
Then beware.

Flamingos gossiping,
Watching elephants race,
Sea lions balancing balls on their heads,
See the lions have great big fights.

Never, ever go to the zoo at night,
There are animals everywhere.
If you don't want to get a fright,
Then beware.

Watch tigers dream sleeping,
See giraffes eat off high trees.
See the monkey hang upside down from trees
And listen to gorillas bang their chests.

Never ever go to the zoo at night,
There are animals everywhere.
If you don't want to get a fright,
Then beware.

Julian Lewis (10)
Jesson's CE Primary School

Eternal Whale

Huge, strong, mighty
Like a gigantic shark
Like a massive target
A direct hit makes me sad
Something no one cares about
It reminds me how sad their death can be.

Emma Seddon (10)
Jesson's CE Primary School

Tigers

Fur for our feathery carpets,
Bones for our medicine.

The glowing of a tiger,
So alert.
Tigers we heard you, calling us,
It was like a vibrating drill,
Don't kill!

Fur for our feathery carpets,
Bones for our medicine.

We could see your colourful skin,
Orange and black, smooth and fluffy,
But we still heard you,
Calling, calling,
I could still see you falling.

Fur for our feather carpets,
Bones for our medicine.

I could still see you,
There beside me,
Still calling me, howling and growling.

Carla Fereday (11)
Jesson's CE Primary School

If I Was!

If I was a dolphin I would go for a swim,
Of course not when the sky goes dim.
If I was a fish I would be colourful and bright,
Almost everything would give me a fright.
If I was a spider I would walk quite slow,
When somebody came past I would go on the low.
If I was a bird I would flap my wings,
Fly in the sky, do all kinds of things.
My wings would be light as a feather,
Then I'll always get caught in the weather.

Jaspreet Ghataora (11)
Jesson's CE Primary School

Danger, Danger

Singing:
Reminds me of whales,
Splishing, splashing with their tails,
Like a whirling tornado,
Like a swirling volcano,
In the ocean water, getting deeper and deeper,
They freely swim,
Someone shooting, dying, hurting them,
Danger . . .
Danger . . .
Unseen . . .

Cold:
Misty, foggy, snowy - breezy, chilly, shivering,
The white large creatures emerging from snow,
Polar bears,
We hear them cry, we hear their fear,
Like a mighty ball of snow,
Like a frozen block of ice.
Humans making them lonely, parted, hurting them.
Danger . . .
Danger . . .
Helpless . . .

Dullness:
Reminds me of the colour of elephants,
A herd of tumbling feet,
In the cold water lake, where they gather and meet,
Like a foam of fluffy cloud,
Like a soaring star! Together all safe.
Us, making them die and forgotten.
Danger . . .
Danger . . .
Out of sight . . .

Sabrina Rahman (11)
Jesson's CE Primary School

The Whale

I sit and wait, I see nothing
I sit and listen, I hear you calling
Calling for help
Splash, splash in the sea
Trying to get away
The poachers are coming

Swimming in the sea
Faster and faster
Trying to get away
Calling and calling
Calling for help
They get closer and closer

They get you
They grab you
They shoot you
You're no longer calling
You're no longer splashing
All is still.

Daniel Williams (11)
Jesson's CE Primary School

Whale

Whale
Giant and glorious whales
Unimaginable whales
Marvellous, impressive and superb
Yelling for its life
Feeling desperate
Fabulous whales
Whales
Remind us to be desperate for life.

Alan Kayinamura (10)
Jesson's CE Primary School

The Panda

The almighty panda
White and black
A wonderful ball of fluff
Immeasurable black eyes
How could you harm such a thing?
Go away pick on someone else
You great big bully
The panda would never do such a thing
Think about it
Its lands are in danger, no bamboo!
What could the panda do to you?
You steal his bamboo
He will steal your chips
Think about it!

Daniel King (10)
Jesson's CE Primary School

Tigers

Tigers
Innocent creatures of God
Yet man will go against his law
And let him die for me
Radiant, sunny and cheerful
If I did not take pills, he would not be dead

He's surrounded, he can't move
Next time I see him he will be my rug
Help! He roars, don't let me die
You need pills, I need not to die!

It's over now, shut your eyes and die
Don't make me feel so bad
Because my kind did this to you.

Victoria Astley (10)
Jesson's CE Primary School

Dolphins!

Dolphins are intelligent creatures,
They love to swim in the sea,
Their colour is silvery and slate-grey.

They swim in the sea looking confident,
They live to be in the sea,
They are underwater angels.

They spring out of the sea,
Bouncing and leaping,
They jump back into the sea.

Dolphins make me feel excited,
They make me feel heartbroken,
They swim exceedingly, amazingly fast.

Dolphins swim gracefully,
They dive into the ultramarine sea,
Jumping very emotionally.

Dolphins remind me of all the creatures in the world!

Laura Chambers (10)
Jesson's CE Primary School

Whales!

Whales are exquisite creatures
They swim around in the ocean
They leap out of the water
Like a spring comes out of a bed
And topple into the water
When it is swimming around
Its heart goes faster and faster
Whales are clever - they know everything
So there it is, the star of the ocean.

Lahtara Kiffin (11)
Jesson's CE Primary School

Tiger

Tiger, a magnificent creature growling by day
But silent at night
A mighty tiger also huge and strong
Being hunted for fur coats
And that is a silly thing

Like a protective mother
Making sure its cubs are safe
It makes me sad to know baby cubs
And mother tigers are being killed

Like a tiny person it makes me feel depressed
Tiger - there might be no tigers left
It reminds me of death, then we're gone.

David Johal (11)
Jesson's CE Primary School

Whales

Dying
Intelligent, graceful, stylish
A floating elephant in the sea
Like a swimming church
It makes me feel how exceedingly small humans are
I feel like a bee that no one sees
Whales
It makes me think of how
Substantial whales are.

Nicholas Rushton (10)
Jesson's CE Primary School

Whales

Whales are breathtaking
Whales are right
Whales are sparkling
Even at night

Whales are extensive
Whales are vast
Whales have wisdom
And are extremely fast

They are very sensible
They are highly royal
They are remarkably jumbo
And truly loyal!

Kelly Holness (10)
Jesson's CE Primary School

Whales!

Whales are wise,
They have a mighty size,
We catch them with a harpoon
And maybe they will all be gone soon.

Whales, whales!
Help them live,
Their mighty size
Is what makes them wise,
So don't use your harpoon
Just to kill one soon.

Beverley Cox (11)
Jesson's CE Primary School

Giant Pandas

I'm so hungry,
Where is my bamboo?
I've searched for ages,
My brothers and sisters have died of starvation,
I don't eat anything else,
Only if I did,
I would not be in this mess,
I'm lost in a nature wonderland!

Is all this my fault?
I don't understand,
What will happen to me in the next few years
Or even the next few months and days?
My life is a misery.

Larcinda Yale (10)
Jesson's CE Primary School

Whales

Whales
Intelligent creatures
Enormous, gigantic, mighty
Like a crashing mountain
Like a floating castle
I'm a midget compared to a whale
Whales
Floating through the ocean silently
Some sing, some don't
The harpoon floating like a missile in the air
Ready to hit them with a scare.

Adrian Hyatt (11)
Jesson's CE Primary School

The White Creature

Playing in the snow,
See how fast he could go,
Catching fish from the sea,
How nice that could be.

With white wavy fur,
He roars out a big grrrr,
He leaves prints with his paws,
While protecting with his claws.

The white creature does not care
About the animals that he snares,
Along the snowy hills he investigates,
Back to his cave in winter he hibernates.

Christopher Hubbard (10)
Jesson's CE Primary School

Whales!

Whales
Are enormous, warm-blooded mammals,
Wise, wonderful, gigantic,
Like an almighty mountain,
Like a gigantic tower,
It makes me depressed,
Because whales are dying,
I heard them singing
For their lives.

Stephen Hill (10)
Jesson's CE Primary School

The Suffering Whale

Suffering, the whale tries to get out of the net,
Singing its song for the last time,
Trying to call other whales to help it,
Crying and striving for their safety,
'Let me out,' they screech,
People calling out saying, 'I've got a whale.'
The other whales watching on in fright
And looking in disgust
And then it's the end for the whale.

Myles Nettleford (10)
Jesson's CE Primary School

Dolphin

The sparkling dolphin,
Gigantic mammal,
Tremendous, magnificent,
Like an angel glowing in the water,
Like a shooting star underwater,
Which gets you broken-hearted every time,
Like something that never lets you down,
The sparkling dolphin,
Reminds us that it's our fault
They die.

Ataf Iqbal (11)
Jesson's CE Primary School

A Starry Night

I think I see a sparkling star,
But, oh my, it's so very far
Oh I wish I could climb that high
To see it with my very own eye
I wish I could see
That very special star
So close to my heart
I'll treasure it forever like a diamond
In my room watching over me
By night, by night.

Natasha Malcolm (11)
Jesson's CE Primary School

Seasons

Snowball fights, a kid's delight,
The crystal-topped bark, where the birds sing their lark,
Birds natter, as teeth chatter,
This is the season of winter.

Daffodils bloom, the sun will be here soon,
New lambs arrive, very active and alive,
The Easter bunny pops out to say hello
And leaves you an egg so you will know,
This is the season of spring.

Seaside time is here again, will we go on a plane?
The people at the barbecue shout, 'Let's get the paddling pool out.'
Ice creams melt as the temperature is felt,
This is the season of summer.

Leaves come tumbling down, orange, red and brown,
Woodpeckers out to play, bare trees are here to stay,
Bonfire Night, will the fireworks give us a fright?
This is the season of autumn.

Zoe Parkinson (10)
Newfield Park Primary School

Snow

A fluffy white blanket that covers the world,
The wool of a sheep sheared and curled.
Snowmen stand sturdy and tall,
Snowballs that whizz, no target at all!
A wintry wonderful down from the sky,
A playground of a lifetime for you and I!

A great orange in the fruit bowl of blue,
Thaws out the fluffy white blanket that covered the world,
The wool of that sheep, sheared and curled.
The snowmen that stood so sturdy and tall,
The snowballs that whizzed, no target at all.
That playground of a lifetime for you and I,
Our winter wonderland, back up to the sky . . .

Emma Gregory (10)
Newfield Park Primary School

Winter

Icicles hang like teardrops from window frames,
While warm fires glow contently beyond them,
A soft white duvet of snow covers the town gently,
My coat, hat, scarf and gloves are waiting on the radiator to be worn,
Not as many animals are being seen since they are hibernating,
Snowflakes fall like small, white doves from the heavens,
My hands are red raw and numb with the cold,
The days are slowly getting shorter as the nights are
slowly getting longer,
All the birds have flown south for this season,
All these sightings could mean only one thing,
Winter is here.

Roseanna Dunham (10)
Newfield Park Primary School

My Greatest Fear

My greatest fear has eight legs,
It likes to crawl on clothes pegs,
Its body is small, its legs are long,
If you like them, I've proved you wrong,
It's not a tarantula, it likes the dark
And it's not as happy as a lark,
It is pathetic to be scared of them,
It mainly crawls on a flower stem,
In autumn it's a common sight,
To get rid of them try shining a light,
It likes to crawl on your shoulder,
You won't be scared of them when you're older,
It doesn't like to get a suntan,
For my greatest fear is spider harvestman!

Jake Ingram (11)
Newfield Park Primary School

Summer

Summer means the sand,
While listening to the band.
Summer is the sea,
Children shout with glee.
While you wear your sunglasses,
You will hear water splashes.
Many people eat ice cream,
While having a dreamy dream.
It can mean a lot of hassle,
To build a massive sandcastle.

Luke Spooner (11)
Newfield Park Primary School

My Magic Monster

My magic monster will have a large head
And will be what everyone dreads
Sharp claws
And will do frightful roars
It will be very tall
And will eat anything at all
It will have sharp teeth
And will be a thief
My magic monster

My magic monster will have huge wings
And will collect all kinds of things
It will have lots of gold
And will not do anything it's told
It will have pointy ears
And will never shed any tears
It will have brown fur
Lovely hair
My magic monster

My magic monster will have a long tail
And will not be as slow as a snail
It can run like the wind
And shows five rows of teeth when it grins
It will have red eyes
Never fear when it dies
It will fly like an eagle
And will eat lots of beagles
My magic monster.

James Bishop (11)
Newfield Park Primary School

My Dream Poem

I dream of fishing on the vast ocean blue,
To catch a blue marlin would be good, or even two,
I love the waves as they crash on the shore,
The spray of the sea horses as they fight their war,
Can anyone beat the anger of the sea?
No, I don't think so, not even me!

The fishermen daily go out in their boats,
Wearing brightly coloured fishing coats,
Oh what a life it must be!
Young, fit and fancy free!

They bring home their catch every night,
How many fish have taken the bite!
People rush to see what they've caught,
The fish are taken to shops, ready to be bought.

What I would give to be one of these men,
Earning their living catching fish six, eight, maybe ten,
Wives sit at home waiting for news,
Hoping the boats return and their crews.

You never know the strength of the sea,
One minute calm, next covering me!
Children play happily in the soft, golden sand,
Fishermen thankful when they sight land.

Always be warned the sea can be mean,
Be careful and enjoy, but remember stay keen.

David Jones (11)
Newfield Park Primary School

A Weird Day!

I went to school unaware
That this was the day
Yes, the very day
Where things would go weird

I saw a mouse
Go up to a house
Then the house
Ran away from the mouse
On that weird day

I got to school
But it had eaten a pool
Then someone with a stool
Came and thought he was cool
On that weird day

When I went home
I found the dome
Under gallons of foam
Just so it could go on loan
On that weird day

I put on the TV
And then in came a bee
It said to me
'I've bought you a fee'
On that weird day

I went to bed
And then my ted
Came and said
'Can I sleep on your head?'
On that weird day

Or was it a dream?

Ryan Tromans (10)
Newfield Park Primary School

A Kenning About The Lion

A glory gobbler
A rageful roarer
A ravenous ruler
A royal reigner
A proud predator
A beastly boaster
A boasting biter
A fearful fighter.

Jessica Pang (10)
Newfield Park Primary School

A Rabbit

A carrot muncher
A grass cruncher
A fluffy mound
A leap and a bound
A little hopper
A currant dropper
A hay snuggler
A child hugger.

Natasha Ewers (11)
Newfield Park Primary School

Summer

The sun sparkling on the clean, clear water
As the old lady stood waiting for her daughter
The sun was as hot as a ball of burning fire
The Earth cried out for rain, its one desire
It hasn't rained for days
But the sun still beats down with its rays.

Zoë Baldwin (9)
Olive Hill Primary School

The Substitute Teacher

My teacher's gone on holiday
I didn't mean to scare her away
Hey, a substitute this will be fun
I'll sit by Toni, she's my best chum

We'll play pranks
Flying frogs, whoopee cushion
Glue and feathers on the door
This will be fun after all

Her name's Miss Hall
And she's really small
She's really very old
And she treats you like a 16-year-old

Tests every day
School's such a bore
And that's not it *all!*

Rachel Manley (10)
Olive Hill Primary School

Hallowe'en

Bring a lantern,
Bring a light,
It must be
Hallowe'en tonight.

I saw a pixie,
Small and fine,
Hanging off a
Washing line.

I saw a fairy,
Who was very small
And a big-eyed giant,
About ten feet tall.

Ammarah Iqbal (9)
Olive Hill Primary School

Haikus

Spring
Seen the buds sprouting
Daffodils on the green grass
And I watch them grow

Summer
Lying in the sun
While the daffodils spring up
I like the summer

Autumn
Leaves sway in the wind
Leaves are drifting to the ground
Autumn, nice season

Winter
Snow falls from Heaven
Snow glistening in the sun
I love winter snow!

Amie Watson (10)
Olive Hill Primary School

Spring

Spring is nearly here
Let's all shout and cheer
Flowers will be blooming
The lawn will soon need grooming

Lambs will soon be born
Farmers plant their corn
Nights stay lighter for longer
Baby animals get stronger

We all start thinking about the summer ahead
Sitting on the patio before we go to bed
Cheers to spring and all that it brings!

Bethany Westbury (8)
Olive Hill Primary School

About Our Teacher

We go to school every day,
It's kind of nice in a way.

Our teacher is called Mrs Willets,
She shouts at us every minute.

She's so glad,
But a bit mad.

She's never there,
We don't care.

She has straight hair
And she goes to the fair.

She cleans her classroom
With her sparkly broom.

She likes reading books
And she's got the looks.

We think she is nice,
Like Mrs Price.

She never says it twice,
She likes mice.

We think she is kind,
But she's not blind.

Laila Mohsen & Munira Gul (10)
Olive Hill Primary School

The Dice

Double one,
Snakes' eyes!
You always get
Something,
When you roll the dice.

Shake them up,
See what you get,
Numbers, numbers!
Why don't you bet?

Take a chance,
Roll the dice,
You may get a six,
That would be nice!

Chinkety, chink!
What a game!
When you lose,
It's such a pain.

Have you won?
Let me see!
Oh me, oh my,
What fun!

Take a chance,
Roll the dice,
You may get a six,
That would be nice!

Christopher Jackson (10)
Olive Hill Primary School

Joy Of Christmas

Glancing out of the window,
I see the elegant blanket of snow,
Glistening and untouched,
Very well, I know,
For all the lights down our road
Have all been switched on,
Now Christmas cheer has really begun.

Suddenly the day has crept upon us
And excitement floods the streets,
We wait with baited breath
For Christmas things like sweets and presents,
Time to go to bed,
Time to say goodnight
And close my eyes, but not too tight!

Rosie Dodds (10)
Olive Hill Primary School

Animal Antics

Ants like eating very good pears
Bears like beer with chocolate éclairs
Cats like wearing nice warm mittens
Female cats like having kittens
Dogs like going for a walk in the park
Hamsters like living in the dark
Dinosaurs like cutting with scissors
Giraffes like having school dinners
Beavers like eating their peas
Badgers don't like getting stung by bees
Sheep like eating grass
Zebras are very holy and go to Mass
Lions like going to a fancy dress ball
But bears aren't so keen, so wait in the hall.

Claire Byrne (8)
Our Lady & St Kenelm School

Untitled

It is spring, it makes even more flowers grow
And grows strawberries too
And you can sit outside and listen to the birds singing
It is spring

It is summer, the sunshine is shining on all the flowers
Making them grow
It is also making people have a tan too
It is summer

It is autumn, the leaves are falling off the trees
Because they need to breathe and have a sneeze
They spin and twirl, it is like little dancing fairies in the sky
It is autumn

It is winter, the snow is thick and soft
You can easily make a snowman with that
You can play snowball fights too
I get my presents and Merry Christmas.

Alice Grennan (7)
Our Lady & St Kenelm School

Valentines

Every boy and girl I meet,
I think they are so sweet.
Every day when I pray,
I am giving love away.
Every day your dreams come true,
I am giving my life to you.
The Lord prepares a feast for us,
We enjoy it when we must.
Now we are married,
Just to be one happy family.

Megan & Rebecca Ingram (8)
Our Lady & St Kenelm School

The Netballer!

I pull on my netball skirt, quivering
Panic-stricken - about to face my greatest fear!
Going through tactics in my head, distantly
I hear an enthusiastic cheer -
Coming on to the pitch, the seating explodes
With eager applause, shouting with anticipation;
Slowly into position; the whistle blows!
Look, the ball is approaching me,
My sweaty hands clutch it -
I pass frantically! . . . We are advancing
Towards the shooting area, dodging tackles,
Weeks of practising could now pay off,
Will we score? Could it be me?
Knees bent, I shoot, the ball rolls around the rim of the net,
Will I score a fabulous goal?
I shall never know, too soon I'm back to reality,
For the hundredth time I wake in suspense,
Was I the netball star?

Catherine Higgins (10) & Esther Olive (9)
Our Lady & St Kenelm School

Untitled

Autumn is going in a day
There is not much to say
Winter is coming soon
It will probably be snowing in the afternoon
Come on, get your hats out
Go inside and scream and shout
Snow is drifting on the ground
Don't be silly and run around.

Francesca Collins (8)
Our Lady & St Kenelm School

The Dancer

I put on my wig and leap about
Dancing like a fairy with my shiny dance shoes on
The adjudicator's thoughts, I don't know yet
All my worries will soon be gone -

I hear boys' shoes clicking
I see girls' wigs waving
The excitement is coming
My luck is saving
For a few more minutes -
I shall never know whether I win or lose
Too soon I am back in the same old boring dance class
In the ordinary world.

Fae Doherty & Francesca Rollason (9)
Our Lady & St Kenelm School

The Singer

I put on my make-up ready to sing,
Exploring the magic of singing,
The beat of the music, *I rock my body*,
On and on I dance.

I listen to people cheering,
I feel like I'm going to burst,
The tune of the music,
I stamp my feet.

Suddenly I hear fireworks exploding just for me,
Then I feel confetti running down my body,
I won the competition,
Yeah!

Laura Breen & Florence Astley (10)
Our Lady & St Kenelm School

The Teacher

I put on my laptop and plan,
Sitting marking the books,
The secrets of teaching,
On and on I mark.

At nine o'clock the children come in like elephants,
Working hard, pens writing,
Down steps to get to the playground,
Look, children in detention,
No, it's only chairs.

Back to the classroom,
Does that drawer hold my red pen
Or some old maths books?

I shall never know,
Too soon I wake up,
I'm in the car ready to get out to college,
Training as a teacher.

Amie Jones (9)
Our Lady & St Kenelm School

The Painter

I select my brush and paint,
Visualising my drawing,
On a blank white page, around my creative brain,
I think more and more -
Over vast seas to green pastures,
Honeybees settle in flowers doing their jobs,
Over stingrays that vanish in the sand,
Look, the pictures are alive,
They stare at me -
It was just my imagination - does that tree
Home some birds that chirp and tweet?

But I shall never know, too soon someone shouts,
'You won't get any money if you daydream, me lad!'
Back I go to the plain old wall, with my brush and paint.

Amy Chan (10)
Our Lady & St Kenelm School

Cinderella

There once was a girl, very pretty,
Who slept in a coal cellar, hard and gritty
And her life was full of pity,
Poor girl!

She always had to do hard labour,
For her stepsisters, her they did not favour,
Because she was a lot more abler,
Poor girl!

She lived in a world full of chores,
Battles, fighting, hatred and wars
And people were always breaking the laws,
Poor girl!

Then, one day, a henchman tall
Came in with an important call,
The king and prince were having a ball,
Wowee!

But Cinders was invited not,
So extra chores there were a lot,
Her whole life was in a knot,
Poor girl!

On the night of the ball, while most were sleeping,
Cinders was miserably weeping
And in the kitchen she was gently sweeping,
Poor girl!

But suddenly a light appeared,
Cinderella quickly reared,
But still the light slowly neared,
Poor girl!

An old lady was standing there,
Suddenly the room seemed bare,
Both hearts seemed to share,
Poor girl!

The lady said, 'Do not fear!
There's a good reason why I'm here,
You're going to the ball, my dear!'
What a nice lady!

'Now darling, fetch me some mice,
That's right! Sugar and spice and all things nice,
Turn them into horses!'
What a nice lady.

Then she made carriages, then a handsome footman
And then she made Cinderella look like a beautiful woman,
What a nice lady!

But it wasn't all bliss,
For the old lady said this,
'For you girl, I have a warning,
Return home the hour before morning!'

Then Cinderella did arrive
And suddenly felt alive,
The prince and she danced
And around the room they pranced.
Wowee!

Then suddenly the clock struck midnight,
Cinderella jumped up with fright,
'I have to leave right now, tonight!'
Oh dear!

Cinderella did not feel glad,
No, indeed, she felt quite sad,
In fact, she felt so bad!
Oh dear!

They said the night before there was a disaster,
There was no happily ever after,
The prince's love disappeared after
The ball!

The slipper Cinders did try on,
The prince she had indeed won!
Oh joy, oh joy, joy everyone!
Now let us all go 'aw' together!
Awww!

Miranda Jones (10)
Our Lady & St Kenelm School

A Morning In The Country

A morning in the country is so pleasant and so dear,
The deer in the forest grazes silently,
A morning in the country is one of the best places to be,
The swift and silent singing,
One bird or even more, start singing in the treetops,
A morning in the country is a lovely place to be,
Go down the lane and there you will see,
A pheasant crossing the road,
Sheep in the field munching up the grass,
Calves drinking milk,
Horses galloping along the road,
When finally all the animals start to doze,
The sun starts to set in the west,
Now all is dark and calm,
Owls hooting in the trees,
Foxes come out and play,
Under the moonlit sky,
After a joyful night,
The sun starts to rise,
Owls, foxes go back to their homes,
The other animals come out and play,
So come to the country, it's a lovely place to be.

Alice Claronino (8)
St Alphege CE Junior School, Solihull

Mum And Dad

M y mummy is the best in the world,
U nspeakably nice Mummy is,
M y dad is great,
M y parents are cool,
Y ou will agree of course that parents are the best.

Sarah Vanhouse (8)
St Alphege CE Junior School, Solihull

I Want

I want a hamster
But my mum says I can't have one
'Cause they are hard to look after
And I'll never clean it out

I want a monkey
But my mum says I can't have one
'Cause they swing about and we'll
Never get any peace

I want a gerbil
But my mum says I can't have one
'Cause the cage will be too much money
And I'll only want the biggest

I want a gorilla
But my mum says I can't have one
'Cause they're too big
And he'll never fit in the house

I want a rabbit
But my mum says I can't have one
'Cause she doesn't want a pet in the garden
And they'll make her eyes itchy.

Jessica Homer (8)
St Alphege CE Junior School, Solihull

The Sea

Her hair was a wave of highlighted white and blue
Her voice, a whale's melody
Her eyes a radiant blue
Her hands are full of tropical fish
Her body stretches across the world
Coming and going here and there.

Roxanne Steeley (10)
St Alphege CE Junior School, Solihull

Summer Holidays

The sun is shining,
Life is fun!
Children playing,
No homework to be done!

Trips to the seaside,
Sandcastles being made,
It is getting very hot now,
We really need to find some shade!

Swimming in the ocean,
Looking out to sea,
Many kinds of fish,
Swimming next to me!

Lazy days in the park,
Picnics by the stream,
Not a care in the world,
This can only be a dream!

Thomas Biddle (8)
St Alphege CE Junior School, Solihull

Myself!

I go up the stairs
Nothing
I look around
Nothing
I go back down
Nothing
Wait
Yes, it's a shadow
I may be nothing to my friends
So they say with glee
But to myself I'm
Me!

Seraphina Neville (10)
St Alphege CE Junior School, Solihull

The Fairy Charm

Page of book, pen and paper,
Turn this person into vapour.

Poison of snake,
Brain of frog,
Eye of student,
Tongue of dog,
Knowledge of teacher,
Licker of death,
Mane of lion,
Fur of cat.

Page of book, pen and paper,
Turn this person into vapour.

Spot of leopard,
Tail of root,
Head of human,
Toe of frog,
Body of gnat,
Foot of pig,
Scale of snake,
Leg of earwig.

Page of book, pen and paper,
Turn this person into vapour.

Joshua Brampton (11)
St Alphege CE Junior School, Solihull

My Nan's Dog

My nan's dog is called Joe
He is smooth and furry
I like to stroke him
And he wears a big blue bow.

Eleanor Clarke (8)
St Alphege CE Junior School, Solihull

My Mum's A Witch

I think my mum's a witch,
Although I'm still not sure,
She's started growing warts and things
And grey hairs galore.

Her saucepan's like a cauldron,
She boils it all day long,
I dread to think what's in it,
It might be a toad's tongue.

She's also started muttering things,
I think they could be spells,
She could be planning to cook me,
That would cause some smells!

Oh no! She's coming towards me,
I think I'm going to scream,
Somebody help me quick! . . .
Phew, it was only a dream!

Rory McMeekin (11)
St Alphege CE Junior School, Solihull

Sport

Sport, sport, sport, it is so good
It is the best, the best,
I wish I was the best at sport -
I wonder if I am?
I can climb high mountains -
High as the heavens.
Run, run, run, fast, fast, fast -
Will I ever catch the wind?
If you were on a trampoline -
Jump as high as you can and touch the stars!
In all sports it's not the winning or the losing -
It's the taking part.

Harpaal Sanghera (7)
St Alphege CE Junior School, Solihull

Spring

Spring is colourful,
Spring is light,
Spring is bright
And all things nice.

I like spring, I like spring,
It is the greatest thing,
I like spring.

I like spring, spring is around,
Spring is there,
Spring is everywhere.

I love spring!

Birds singing in the trees,
Dancing daffodils in the breeze.
The sweet smell of roses in the air.

I love the wonders of . . .
Spring!

Chelsea Gooding (7)
St Alphege CE Junior School, Solihull

Puppies

Puppies can bite
Puppies chase cats
They wag their tails
And sleep on mats

They chew your hair
Fingers and toes
And if you're not careful
They'll chew your nose

But whatever they do
I think they're so cute
I'd rather have a puppy
Than a frog or a newt.

Abigail Clarke (7)
St Alphege CE Junior School, Solihull

School

School, school is so cool
Working hard and having fun
Excellent teachers and fab school meals
Really cool deals
Top trump cards allowed
And any other cards you can think of

Number one playground
Huge and full of laughter
Everyone is nice
You can bring your own snack
And bring your own lunch
Then the afternoon's here
And brings with it art, craft
And design and technology
After that, school's finished
And my poem's finished too.

James Stout (8)
St Alphege CE Junior School, Solihull

We Are All Equal

We are all equal
Brown, black and white
Being a certain colour
Doesn't make us wrong or right

We are all equal
Muslim, Christian, Jew
Whatever our religion
Doesn't change me and you

We are all equal
Young, old, rich and poor
It's not what's on the outside
The inside matters more!

Evie Farmer (9)
St Alphege CE Junior School, Solihull

Colours!

Colours dull,
Colours bright,
Colours are a lovely sight!

They make patterns on your walls
And sometimes even on balls.

Colours dull,
Colours bright,
Colours are a lovely sight!

Colours are the best you have ever seen,
Colours are blue, yellow and green.

Colours dull,
Colours bright,
Colours are a lovely sight!

Colours all around the room,
Colours are like a flower in bloom.

Colours dull,
Colours bright,
Colours are a lovely sight!

Olivia Rawlings (9)
St Alphege CE Junior School, Solihull

Wacky Mad Pants

The wacky kids go out to play,
Going mad all through the day,
Playing a game of wacky tennis,
The winner of the game so far is Dennis,
180 points to 10,
The loser of the game today is Edd,
He worked so hard, he went bright red!

Thomas Clancy (8)
St Alphege CE Junior School, Solihull

Creak!

Creak! Creak!
Creak! Creak!
Something's creaking, we should have it fixed.
But what could it be? I can't be sure.
I've never heard something that creaky before.
It might be a robber moving around,
It might be weeks until I am found.
He will leave my blood on the floor,
He will leave the trail up to the door.
It might be a demon who hides in the dark,
He never fears but has a big black mark.
Maybe it's a goblin that kills for fun,
The only way to escape is to scream and run.
It might be a ghoul who scares for a joke,
Who usually scares the old folk.
He might come up to my bed
And bite off my head.
Now listen carefully my friend,
If you hear creaking, it could be . . .
The end
Unless it's just a creaky floorboard.

Wendy Norman (9)
St Alphege CE Junior School, Solihull

My Life

My life is full of joy.
My life is full of hope.
My life is full of peace.
My life is full of grace.
My life is full of everyone.

Lucy Shenton (10)
St Alphege CE Junior School, Solihull

Henry VIII

Henry who had six wives,
Changed the church for all time.

Catherine of Aragon was wife number one,
She was divorced because she had no son.

Anne Boleyn was Henry's number two,
Her head flew for she had no son too.

Henry fancied Jane Seymour,
She had a son, but was no more.

Anne was as pretty as a picture,
When Henry saw her, he simply ditched her.

Catherine Howard was easily led,
So much so, it was off with her head!

Henry's last was Katherine Parr,
She was his best wife so far.

But now though Henry was so fat and ill,
He couldn't last to make his will.

Alice Montgomery (10)
St Alphege CE Junior School, Solihull

Bees

Bees: they shouldn't be allowed
They are small insects
Buzzing all around.
In and out they fly
As they keep passing by.
I like flies better
They rather like to chill
And also even better
They are easier to kill.

Albert Onyeaka (10)
St Alphege CE Junior School, Solihull

Cats

I like cats, cats are the best,
they don't jump out and be a pest.

L ove and like cats as much as you can do,
you don't say to them 'Go on *shoo!*'
I don't have a cat but you may,
but I think it's worth the pay.
K ittens are furry and cats are furry,
don't get your cat undercontrolled and make it go purry.
E at and eat, let your cat eat
and let it eat lots of meat.

C ats, cats, buy a cat,
because it's better than buying a bat.
A cat is the best, so get one, they are the best
and don't let your cat go north or west.
T ake from the shop and get one
and the best name is Tom.
S o get one
and you will have won!

Hannah Victoria Pittaway (8)
St Alphege CE Junior School, Solihull

Milo

Milo is a ginger cat
who would always chase a rat

He has soft fur
and when he is happy, he will purr

When he is tired he likes to sleep
but when he is lively he likes to leap

When he is asleep he covers his eyes with his paws
and sometimes he even snores!

I love Milo, he is a special fluffy cat
and I don't think anyone would disagree with that.

Beatrice Freeman (8)
St Alphege CE Junior School, Solihull

My Adventure With The Sea

I am a little turtle swimming through the sea,
Oh no! There's a crab running after me.
I glide through the sea speedily to my cave,
I slide in the little hole, being very brave.
I see a lovely jellyfish, ready to be eaten,
I know it's very small; it doesn't want to be beaten.
I go outside my cave and wait just outside my door,
Then I see a big crab jumping on the floor.
Very, very scared, I hurriedly run back in,
I sit on my bed and . . . ouch! a pin.
I curl up in my shell; I look just like a stone,
I can't get up; it feels like I've broken a bone.
I creep out my secret hole and swim to the sand,
I can't bear looking around and then I see the land.

Avneet Johal (11)
St Alphege CE Junior School, Solihull

Milly!

I have a dog called Milly,
She is very silly,
She likes a fuss,
But not a puss.

She wears a hat,
But sits on a mat,
She is grey and lazy,
We think she is very crazy.

She eats my fish,
I even had her for a wish!
I love my Milly,
She's very silly!

Soraya Birch (8)
St Alphege CE Junior School, Solihull

Creak

Something's creaky,
It's really freaky,
It's hiding behind the door,
Now it's creeping up the floor!
It's going to cook me in a bowl,
Then eat me whole!
Or maybe,
It could eat me with cream,
Like in my worst dream!
I don't know what to do,
I feel like going boo hoo!
It's
Scary,
Freaky,
Creaky,
Aaarrrggghh!
(Or it could be my brother getting a drink.)

Anna Fooks (10)
St Alphege CE Junior School, Solihull

What Can You See?

See
What can you see?
The golden rays of the evening sunset
The rippling water of the nearby stream

See
What can you see?
The old oak tree swaying gently in the morning breeze
The happy sight of a newborn baby

See
What can you see?
The early morning snow all sharp and cold
The mid-spring flowers as bright as the sun.

Jessica Cuttriss (8)
St Alphege CE Junior School, Solihull

This Is A Poem About Animals

There's an animal that has claws like daggers
It's black and white
And hunts at night
That's right it's called a badger

There's an animal that is slithery
It's small
It's fast
That's right it's called an asp

There's an animal that is big
It's furry
It's strength is stronger than iron
That's right it's called a lion

There's an animal that is small
It's jumpy
It likes to jump on a log
That's right it's called a frog.

Kieran Daliwal (9)
St Alphege CE Junior School, Solihull

Best Friends

B est friends are always there,
E verywhere, they always care,
S illy games, calling names,
T easing, joking, sharing secrets

F unny faces
R unning races
I love all these things
E veryone playing by the swings
N ever falling out
D ancing, skipping, swimming, sleeping
S o best friends are well worth keeping!

Rebecca Scott (9)
St Alphege CE Junior School, Solihull

Dogs, Dogs, Dogs

Dogs, dogs, dogs are so cute,
They can even play the flute.

Dogs, dogs, dogs are so cool,
Sometimes they play in the pool.

Dogs, dogs, dogs wag their tail,
But when they're sad, they often wail.

Dogs, dogs, dogs go on walks,
But I've never seen one that talks.

Dogs, dogs, dogs' noses are wet,
If they're not, they have to go to the vet.

Dogs, dogs, dogs are the best,
Even when they have a rest.

Bethan Irving (8)
St Alphege CE Junior School, Solihull

My Dog Tilly

I love my Tilly,
She is very silly!
She makes puddles where you walk
And loves to play and talk.

She goes upstairs without us knowing
And takes our clothes and toys
And takes them down to chew on,
I hate it when she does that,
We have to chase her round the garden.

She is cheeky and goes next door
And we need to bribe her with her treat box,
She always knocks over photos
With her feet and with her tail.

I love my Tilly,
She is very silly!

John Scholes (9)
St Alphege CE Junior School, Solihull

My Cat, Josie

My cat was black and white
She used to eat fish
Straight from the dish
She walked on her legs
Like they were pegs
She liked birds to chase
She ran at her fastest pace
She cared about me
More than tea
She was the best cat
She sat on a mat
When she was hungry
When I stroked her fur
She used to purr
When she was old
She must have been cold
When she was a puss
She used to fuss.

Ellie Hargrave (8)
St Alphege CE Junior School, Solihull

Pet Poem

I wish I had a pony
With a coat of dapple-grey
I often think if only
It could be mine one day
But in fact I have a guinea pig
He's small and grey and round
He eats the grass and doesn't dig
And makes a squeaky sound.

Mary Montgomery (8)
St Alphege CE Junior School, Solihull

My Unicorn

At the stroke of midnight,
After a cold frosty day,
A unicorn came to my window
And gave a little neigh!

I climbed on her back as she
Flew into the air,
I'm afraid of heights,
But then I didn't care!

She came back to my window
And said she would come back soon,
But she really had to go,
It would soon be noon.

I'll never forget my unicorn,
Or the day we met,
She was really close to me,
My little secret pet!

Shannon Fisher (10)
St Alphege CE Junior School, Solihull

I Wish

If I had a wish, I wish I could fly,
If I had a wish, I wish I wouldn't lie.

If I had a wish, I wish I could do magic,
If I had a wish, I wish my life wouldn't be tragic.

If I had a wish, I wish no one could die,
If I had a wish, I wish no one would say goodbye.

I wish, I wish, I wish.

Natalie Lewis (11)
St Alphege CE Junior School, Solihull

Time

I lead living things through their evolutionary stages,
I am old as a fossil and as young as a newborn baby,
Slowly sucking boyhood from energetic children,
'Respect your elders,' I say, for they are my children,
I am '$E=MC^2$', I am the universe,
I am time.
I am the wizard of youth and soul,
I'm the one who makes them old,
Using age as a toll,
To the black and evil troll,
Sometimes I take the form of
A wheelchair or pill,
Sweeping life and energy,
Or making good health ill,
But I'm also the stopper of death
And I'm the one whom baby's born,
I also give that one last breath,
So let my soul; it not be torn.

David Lowry (10)
St Alphege CE Junior School, Solihull

Day By Day

Second by second my heart is pounding
Minute by minute there's something sounding
Hour by hour my life is astounding
Day by day my hair grows longer
Week by week my muscles grow stronger
Month by month the more I grow
Year by year the more I know.

Mia Smart (9)
St Alphege CE Junior School, Solihull

Watery Fun

Surfing is good,
First you lie,
Then nudge the waves,
All of a sudden,
You're riding on flames.

This thing is a
Favourite of mine,
I'd like to do it
All the time.

Diving is cool,
In you go,
Head first, feet last,
All of a sudden,
You're moving so fast.

This thing is a
Favourite of mine,
I'd like to do it
All the time.

Swimming is cool,
Kick your legs,
Left arm, then right,
All of a sudden,
You're feeling so light.

This thing is a
Favourite of mine,
I'd like to do it
All the time.

Splashing is fun,
Bash the water,
Without a care,
All of a sudden,
It's everywhere.

These things are
All my best
And after I've done them,
It's good to rest.

Alex Taylor (8)
St Alphege CE Junior School, Solihull

Lessons At School

First lesson's maths
Where we do algebra, great!
Second lesson English
The lesson where we're never late

Then it's playtime
Where we're eating chocolate bars
Playing games and having fun
My favourite chocolate's Mars

Next lesson's French
Bonjour, j'adore French
Then it's PE
Where we play on a bench

Oh, I'm starving
I'm glad it's dinnertime
Where I eat my dinner
Then go, play in the sunshine

Next it's my favourite subject
Music is the *best!*
I like to play with instruments
Music really is the best, much better than the rest!

Now it's
Ease up, tea's up
So it's home time so . . . *run!*

Aroosa Zaidi (10)
St Alphege CE Junior School, Solihull

Dolphins

Dolphins are the best
They never ever rest
That's why they never do
And have the flu

They play and they play
Every single day
They're living in the deep
That's why they never leap

Dolphins think they're fine
That's why they shine
Dolphins are mammals
But it's a shame they haven't seen camels

They like water
In Majorca
Dolphins have fins
But don't have bins

The ships put in pollution
Which causes dilution
Dolphins have brains
But it never rains.

Mehreen Zaidi (9)
St Alphege CE Junior School, Solihull

A Young Boy From Brum

There once was a young boy from Brum
Who liked to feed his large tum
He ate lots of ice cream
And began to scream
Until his cold tongue went all numb.

Thomas Rusher (9)
St Alphege CE Junior School, Solihull

Squeak!

Squeak! Squeak!
Something's squeaking, I'll go take a peek.

But what can it be? I am not sure,
I've never heard squeaking that squeaky before.

It might be a goblin heading for my bed,
Ready to rip off my head.

Goblin boy's beating his drum,
Ready to gulp me down with a gallon of rum.

Now he's staring at me wide-eyed,
He'll take me and bake me and eat me fried.

That goblin's a freak,
That's why I won't peek.

Now that I'm nearly dead,
Never get out of your bed,

Unless, of course, it's a mouse instead.

Luke Boswell (9)
St Alphege CE Junior School, Solihull

School Is Cool

School, school is so cool, we jump in the swimming pool
Cup of tea in the staffroom
Higher, higher, we go to school, must get better,
One day we play,
One day we don't play,
Leaving school is the best part of the day!

Timothy Sawrey (8)
St Alphege CE Junior School, Solihull

The Enchanted Unicorn

A silver wind is blowing,
A spirit is rising up,
An animal with a sparkling horn,
It's the enchanted unicorn.

Galloping through the open sky,
On a cold and frosty night,
Soaring, gliding, so, so high,
Her purple eyes shining bright.

A sparkling land of enchantment,
Where white horses roam free,
An animal with a sparkling horn,
It's the enchanted unicorn.

Something that is wild and free,
It gave us a ride my sister and me,
An animal with a sparkling horn,
It's the enchanted unicorn.

Sophie Thompson (9)
St Alphege CE Junior School, Solihull

Swimming

S plashing in the water is lots of fun.
W ater in the swimming pool makes all of this fun.
I love the swimming pool.
M aking lots of bubbles underwater.
M anaging to swim one length.
I love the swimming pool.
N ever run around in the swimming pool.
G ames in the swimming pool are really fun.

Emma Wilde (7)
St Alphege CE Junior School, Solihull

Months Go Past!

Roses are red, violets are blue
So make all my wishes come true

Leaves are green, squirrels are brown
Autumn has come at last

Sun is shining, wind is blowing
There's a sunset up in the sky

Owls are howling, trees are shivering
Night sky shining like stars

Winter has finally come
Snowflakes are falling in the cold

One more thing to come, it's
Spring!

Judith Kefas (9)
St Alphege CE Junior School, Solihull

Wildlife

Cats crawl
Lions roar
Giraffes are tall
Bears snore

Spiders are hairy
Frogs leap
Sharks are scary
Sloths sleep

Foxes are sneaky
Ants are small
Monkeys are cheeky
But I am tall!

Isobel Hands (8)
St Alphege CE Junior School, Solihull

Joe

Joe is my little brother
But sometimes he can be a little bother
He's a tinker too!
He runs around the house at half-past two!

He plays with his daddy's tools
But he can't swim in pools
He plays with his mummy's make-up and smears it all over his face
And all over the place

He loves to come in my room
And zoom around like a nutter
And makes himself cough and splutter

He loves to go in the garden on a sunny day
And play in the pool all day
Not swimming but splashing and having fun

He plays with the parrots
And sticks his fingers in the cage
They come and snap at him
They think his fingers are carrots

But when he's in bed resting his little head
It's the safest place for him to be.

Holly Avery (9)
St Alphege CE Junior School, Solihull

Does The Goldfish . . . ?

Watching the goldfish in his small and cosy tank,
But does he watch back at me?
I wonder what the goldfish might be thinking,
But does he think at all?
In such a tiny world of his own, he must get bored,
But does he have a mind to let him?

George Spann (10)
St Alphege CE Junior School, Solihull

Winter

With sparkling frost
With shimmering snow
Winter is here
With no temptation to go

Christmas trees are up
With angels on the tops
Turkey for dinner
Instead of pork or lamb chops

Christmas Day so white and crisp
Having a good time all day
Going into night
Not catching a cold would take all your might

Winter is over
And the snow is melting
I never thought I'd see the day
When the sun would be once again shining away.

Stephanie Biddle (10)
St Alphege CE Junior School, Solihull

Candle

The flame, blue at the bottom, yellow at the top,
Wax dripping, drip, drop,
Candle burning down the wick,
All is left is a narrow wax stick.

Lights are dim,
Left no sin,
Blow out the flame,
Who was to blame?

Rachel Stapley (10)
St Alphege CE Junior School, Solihull

Winter

I make the people dress up warm
And I make the birds fly south.
I make the streets go icy
And I make the seas go cold.
I make the days go short
And I make the sky turn grey.
I make the snow for the snowball fight
And I make your fingers numb.
I make the mountains white
And I make you slip and slide.
I make the animals hibernate,
For I control the snow and ice.
I make you shiver in your pyjamas,
For I am *monster winter.*

Neil Marshall (10)
St Alphege CE Junior School, Solihull

Junior School Is Fun

School - school is so cool,
I really like playing football,
It's fun to watch the Apple Band in the hall,
On Fridays Mr Chamberlain comes to the pool,
Mr Newbold - he's so tall,
Mr Ward - he has all the tools,
Mr McLaren - he's so cool,
When Mr Curran's about, we play by the rule,
Thursdays, dance club with Mrs Simms is cool,
If you are naughty you must stand by the wall,
Monday is fab because it's the first day of school.

Brad Carpenter (8)
St Alphege CE Junior School, Solihull

Nature!

Have you ever wondered what it would be like as a tiny ant or a tall tree?

If you look among your fresh green grass
What do you think you'll see?
A snail or a slug?
A flower or a bug?
A wasp or a honeybee?

Flowers and trees,
Ants and bees,
It's all one part of nature to me.

Just think about ants,
Tiny brown ants,
Do you know how strong they are?
Carrying something twice their size
And going so slow and so far.

Flowers and trees
Ants and bees
It's all one part of nature to me.

Watch ladybirds scuttle
Up plants and up trees,
Can't you just smell
The sweet, fresh green leaves?
The rusty brown bark
Covers the trees.

Flowers and trees,
Ants and bees,
It's all one part of nature to me.

Eleanor Jeffrey (8)
St Alphege CE Junior School, Solihull

Help!

He's there behind me,
Help!
I'm going to keep on running,
He's got my key,
He is really cunning,
Help!

He's really scary,
Help!
I'm not going to stop,
He's really hairy,
He's going to give me the chop,
Help!

He's coming in the door,
Help!
I'm going to be dead,
I'll be lying on the floor,
Argh! my head,
Help!

He's around the bend,
Help!
He's getting nearer,
I can't see my friend,
It's even drearier,
Help!

He's started to run,
Help!
My heart is pounding,
Is he just doing this for fun?
It's even more sounding,
Help!

It's a monster,
Help!
I'm going to be caught,
It's not just a thought,
This is the end!
Help!

Benisha Johal (10)
St Alphege CE Junior School, Solihull

Spring

It is spring
The animals are jumping
The blossom is falling
I am getting taller
We are cleaning the house
Including the mouse

The plants are coming
The animals are running
Plants and screaming
Birds are gleaming
Hip, hip, hooray, the winter has gone
Everyone is singing a song.

Joshua Melvin (9)
St Alphege CE Junior School, Solihull

Summer Colours

The sky is blue, the sea is too
The sun is yellow, a happy fellow
The fields are green, a sunny scene
The red flowers glow as their green leaves blow
All these summer colours come and go.

James Pillinger (8)
St Alphege CE Junior School, Solihull

Winter

Tumbling from above like blue stars,
Rain,
Rain,
Crashing, smashing, lashing.

Dropping like grey paper,
Snow,
Snow,
Floating, settling, glistening.

Rattling on the roof like white pebbles,
Hail,
Hail,
Zooming, bouncing, melting.

Joel Davis (7)
St Alphege CE Junior School, Solihull

These Are The Things I Like To Write

A fairy tale
About a big blue whale,
A story
Which you can read for glory,
A riddle
That could sit in the middle,
A joke
Which you can poke,
A song
Which is so long,
Music notes
To help the song I wrote,
These are the things I like to write.

Emily Heartfield (9)
St Alphege CE Junior School, Solihull

School's Out

School's out
Scream and shout
Lots of fun
For everyone
Sit on the beach
Life's a peach
Swim in the sea
Come with me!
The sun gives light
Strong and bright
The sky is blue
So much to do
School's out
Fun
Games
Eat
Drink
Swim
Enjoy
Ahoy!

Eliot Davis (10)
St Alphege CE Junior School, Solihull

Emerging

I walk across my frosty lawn
At the very crack of dawn
The trees are crisp, the pond is cold
The weather warms up, the leaves unfold

It turns to spring and colours appear
All the people are full of cheer
Trees turn green and there is life in the pond
Great lush hills are far beyond.

Elizabeth Adcock (9)
St Alphege CE Junior School, Solihull

Love

Love is in the air
You may not see it
But you might feel it
Because it is always there
Love is sweet, but nowhere near sour
Love is big, red and true
And you will not catch the flu
It makes you feel tingly all around
And love can be any sort of sound
You can love anyone
As long as it is someone
It's not silly to love
It makes you want to fly above
And if they say they cannot go out with you
Just say, maybe someday.

Elliot Gordon (8)
St Alphege CE Junior School, Solihull

Day

Twinkling stars and a full eye moon,
Sun will come not until after noon.

Misty clouds and a pitch-black sky
And a gentle wind that blows a-high.

The pitter-patter of the dripping taps
And the sleeping children with their teddies by their laps.

Soft snowflakes that make a blanket of snow
And three little robins all perched in a row.

Until finally the moon goes away,
Sleeping children awake, it's already come day.

Stephanie Brew (9)
St Alphege CE Junior School, Solihull

Swimming Race!

Starter's gun
Waves crowding
Eyes sore
Arms ache
Legs pumping
Can't go faster
Stitch in my chest
Gasping for a drink
Toes stiff
Sweating
Tummy hurting
Knees stinging
Nearly there
About to collapse!
Crowd screaming
Have to win!
Goggles steamy
The finishing line
Five lengths away
I've won! I've won!

Emma Bromley (9)
St Alphege CE Junior School, Solihull

Friends

F riends are so cool
R unning around together
I n the playground of school
E very day we play games
N ever falling out with each other
D ancing happily in the school hall
S miling all the time.

Gemma Woolley (8)
St Alphege CE Junior School, Solihull

The Old Tree

The old tree in my back garden,
Has leaves as green as peas.

The old tree in my back garden,
Has a nest of swarming bees.

The old tree in my back garden,
Hangs over the lush green grass.

The old tree in my back garden,
Greets me as I pass.

The old tree in my back garden,
Has old wrinkly bark.

The old tree in my back garden,
Can see all the way to the park!

The old tree in my back garden,
Is very special to me.

The old tree in my back garden,
Will remain wild and free.

Ashley Fraser (10)
St Alphege CE Junior School, Solihull

Cats, Cats, Cats

Cats are cute and small
Cats sit on the wall
Cats' eyes are very bright
Cats are black and white
Cats walk round the street
Cats sit on your feet
Cats lick the dish
Cats' fave food is fish
Cats! Cats! Cats!

Tabitha Loose (7)
St Alphege CE Junior School, Solihull

My Cat, Beanie

I have a cat called Beanie,
She really is quite teeny,
Her face is black, her tummy is white,
She really is a pretty sight.

In my garden she chases birds and bees,
But usually ends up at the top of the trees,
She is so nimble and runs so fast,
My little cat is never last.

I love my cat she's very sweet,
Pretty, cute and oh so neat!
At the end of the day she curls up to sleep,
In a little ball and I don't hear a peep.

Charlotte King (9)
St Alphege CE Junior School, Solihull

Rosie And Umbra

Rosie and Umbra are two lovely pups!
Playing together like two balls of fluff.

Rosie yelping for love,
Then there is Umbra, playing tough and tug.

Rosie and Umbra are getting tired,
'Rosie,' said Umbra, 'isn't it basky time?'

Umbra and Rosie are fast asleep,
Cuddling their toy called Leepy Peep.

Rosie and Umbra have woken up,
They are eating their breakfast, so woof, woof, woof.

Alice Roberts & Fenella Wood (9)
St Alphege CE Junior School, Solihull

When A Tornado Comes!

What a mess,
Up and dressed,
When a tornado comes!

Spin around,
Up and down,
When a tornado comes!

Stay inside,
Don't go for a dive,
When a tornado comes!

Run away,
Don't stay,
When a tornado comes!

Yikes,
Don't go and catch some pikes,
When a tornado comes!

Houses blow,
Up and go,
When a tornado comes!

Don't say yum,
Go and run,
When a tornado comes!

Joseph Dunne (7)
St Anne's Catholic Primary School, Sutton Coldfield

Easter

E aster eggs are lovely to eat,
A ngry soldiers arrest Jesus
S urprises on Easter morning,
T he resurrection of Jesus is here,
E aster time is fun,
R abbits have babies, Easter bunnies are born.

Claudia Pocrnic (7)
St Anne's Catholic Primary School, Sutton Coldfield

When The Volcano Rumbles

When the volcano rumbles
Lava comes, people run.

When the volcano rumbles
Frightened faces, don't do up laces.

When the volcano rumbles
Fire spits, with no hits.

When the volcano rumbles
Fire lightens, people are frightened.

When the volcano rumbles
People die, people cry.

When the volcano rumbles
No one says little liar, because there really is a fire.

Jack Humphrey (8)
St Anne's Catholic Primary School, Sutton Coldfield

A Snowy Day

When the snow falls,
You can make a snowman
And put a carrot on it.

When the snow falls,
It goes on your noses
And it goes on your eyelashes.

When the snow falls,
You can play a snowball fight.

When the snow falls,
You can meet your friend
And play a game.

Saranne Huxton (7)
St Anne's Catholic Primary School, Sutton Coldfield

Eight Penguins Skidding On The Ice

(Inspired by 'Ten Little Schoolboys' by A A Milne)

Eight penguins skidding on the ice,
One slipped over and then there were seven.

Seven penguins skidding on the ice,
One lost his balance and then there were six.

Six penguins skidding on the ice,
One cut a thigh and then there were five.

Five penguins skidding on the ice,
One fell over and then there were four.

Four penguins skidding on the ice,
One broke his leg and then there were three.

Three penguins skidding on the ice,
One tumbled over and then there were two.

Two penguins skidding on the ice,
One went flat and then there was one.

One penguin skidding on the ice,
It fell against the wall and then there were none.

Arian Forouhandeh (7)
St Anne's Catholic Primary School, Sutton Coldfield

Our Little Alien

One little dog alien sitting on a wall
It fell off and broke its paw

One little alien out sitting on a branch
It fell off and ripped its pants!

One little alien sitting on a plum
It fell off and broke its bum

One little alien all alone, say goodbye
It's off to the planet Zone.

Stephanie Graydon (7)
St Anne's Catholic Primary School, Sutton Coldfield

When The Snow Falls

When the snow falls,
People are cold, they put on their hats.

When the snow falls,
It is lovely to watch, even in flats.

When the snow falls,
Snowball fights, snowmen built.

When the snow falls,
Beware it's slippy, *beware* on skates.

When the snow falls
Inside is an oven
Outside is so cool.

Corrine Hughes (7)
St Anne's Catholic Primary School, Sutton Coldfield

I Do That!

I wear caps,
When I read maps.

I play football,
Before I go to the mall.

When I'm in New York,
I eat pork.

It is dark,
When I go to the park.

In the sun,
An elephant weighs a ton.

Connal Trueman (7)
St Anne's Catholic Primary School, Sutton Coldfield

When The Bell Rings

When the bell rings
Chairs clatter, children chatter.

When the bell rings
Children hurry, parents worry.

When the bell rings
Trays away, then we pray.

When the bell rings
Bags and bags, Mum is in rags.

When the bell rings
We get our scarves, then get in our cars.

When the bell rings
Most people yell, others shout!

Lucy Myatt (8)
St Anne's Catholic Primary School, Sutton Coldfield

Five Little Bluebirds

Five little bluebirds sitting on a door
One fell off, then there were four

Four little bluebirds sitting on a tree
One said bye, then there were three

Three little bluebirds standing on a tree
One said boo, then there were two

Two little bluebirds there on a tree
One said look, then there was one

One little bluebird all alone because his friends had gone
He flew away and then there were none.

Matthew O'Doherty (7)
St Anne's Catholic Primary School, Sutton Coldfield

The Seasons

Spring is the best
Better than all the rest
Soaking and blossoming

Winter windy and winter wet
Cold and rainy
Soaking wet

Summer sun and summer go
Summer woes and smelly toes
I just wish the sun could go

Autumn leaves I like the best
They flutter round
In a twist.

Eleanor Regan (8)
St Anne's Catholic Primary School, Sutton Coldfield

Weather Poem

Winter snow, winter glow
Winter glow, winter show
Winter show, winter low
Winter low, winter low
Winter low, winter low

Summer sun, summer hot
Summer burn, summer gun
Summer done, summer gun
Eating ice creams in the sun
Summer, summer
Summer, summer
Summer, summer sun.

Ali Ghaemmaghami (8)
St Anne's Catholic Primary School, Sutton Coldfield

Ten Little Robins

(Inspired by 'Ten Little Schoolboys' by A A Milne)

Ten little robins sitting on the fence
One flew away then there were nine

Nine little robins sitting on the fence
One went whoosh and then there were eight

Eight little robins sitting on the fence
One fell off and then there were seven

Seven little robins sitting on the fence
One went bang and then there were six

Six little robins sitting on the fence
One landed in the bush then there were five

Five little robins sitting on the fence
One went pop and then there were four

Four little robins sitting on the fence
One went plop and then there were three

Three little robins sitting on the fence
One went flap and then there were two

Two little robins sitting on the fence
One fell off and then there was one

One little robin sitting on the fence
One went zoom and then there were none.

Lauren Staley (8)
St Anne's Catholic Primary School, Sutton Coldfield

Summer

S ummer is the best season of them all
U nder umbrellas we sit
M y dad goes and gets a tan
M y ice cream melts
E very day I go to the beach
R iding my bike as the sun sets.

Tom Bannister (8)
St Anne's Catholic Primary School, Sutton Coldfield

Five Scary Vikings

(Inspired by 'Ten Little Schoolboys' by A A Milne)

Five scary Vikings
Climbing up the Sphinx
One tumbled off
And then there were four

Four scary Vikings
Doing eight winks
One missed one out
And then there were three

Three scary Vikings
Breathing in air
One did not
And then there were two

Two scary Vikings
Saying it's not fair
One said it was
And then there was one

One scary Viking
Tying a rope
He did it wrong
And then there were none.

Callum Riley (7)
St Anne's Catholic Primary School, Sutton Coldfield

A Tidal Wave

When a tidal wave hits;
Better run, stop what you're doing before it's too late.

When a tidal wave hits;
No time for surfing, get on your board, surf back to shore.

When a tidal wave hits;
No time for reading, put your books down, follow the crowd.

Thomas McNulty (8)
St Anne's Catholic Primary School, Sutton Coldfield

Winter Into Spring

Geese flying enjoying the weather
They have never lost one single feather

Scarves fluttering in the air
A child eating a juicy pear

Adults walking in the park
Dogs barking when it turns dark

When it's morning people awake
Working dads never have a break

Rainy days come and go
Sad children can't see the snow

Turns spring very quickly
Also the bushes turn very prickly

Very mild today
At least it's not raining like yesterday!

Chloe O'Connor (9)
St Anne's Catholic Primary School, Sutton Coldfield

Tornadoes

Round and round, up and down,
When a tornado comes.

There's such a mess,
When a tornado comes.

People run, there is no sun,
When a tornado comes.

It spins and spins, until it goes,
Into the ground!

Michael Swift (8)
St Anne's Catholic Primary School, Sutton Coldfield

The Seasons Of The Year

Spring is the first season of the year,
Flowers first start to pop up,
Cold winters turn to spring,
We see snowbells and now we are free!

Summer is the season
When we like to go somewhere,
We play and we have fun!

Autumn is the time
To play and jump in the leaves,
Let's have fun.

Winter is the time
We get excited,
Christmas is near,
Have fun in the snow.

Talor Whitham (8)
St Anne's Catholic Primary School, Sutton Coldfield

Winter

Frozen lakes with ghostly snow,
Glittering ice and a frosty glow,
Woolly scarves with matching hats,
In the street no dogs or cats.
Going to school with shivering knees,
There's nothing colder than Mum's keys,
Footprints with crunchy snow,
Everyone's cold of course you know.
Frost on shivering cars,
In the park some icy bars,
Heating on to warm you up,
Time for some tea in a nice red cup.

Anna-Maria Kotulski (8)
St Anne's Catholic Primary School, Sutton Coldfield

Seasons

Spring, a fresh new start,
Saying beautiful from your heart.
Flowers coming up today,
Children going out to play.

Summer is the best of all,
When everybody plays volleyball.
Sunbathing in the sun,
Everyone I see is having fun.

Autumn leaves red, yellow and brown,
Falling, falling, falling down.
Foggy, misty like a grey bee,
It is so near I can't see.

Winter wonderland a frosty bite,
I'm so sure it's icy white.
I love having snowball fights,
Maybe I might . . . alright!

Victoria Stubbs (8)
St Anne's Catholic Primary School, Sutton Coldfield

Lightning

I struck a boy walking along,
Seeing some screaming I try,
A misty shadow I saw along the ground,
Ghostly white the people's faces were,
I hurried and scurried across the town,
Still deserted no one found,
A petrifying scream could be heard,
A horizontal sight, I could have been seen,
I crossed over the dark and foggy hills,
I hit the churchyard, black and dull,
Still I do not even care,
I've been on my adventure, I've finished . . . for now.

Henry Bath (8)
St Anne's Catholic Primary School, Sutton Coldfield

Summer

Swimming in the sun
Making sandcastles
Eating ice cream
Playing football on the beach
Playing with the dinghy in the water
Watching the sun go down
Sunbathing in the sun
Having water fights in the sea
Making a sand boat
Playing catch in the sea
Collecting seashells
Watching the boats go past
Climbing the rocks.

Conor Flaherty (8)
St Anne's Catholic Primary School, Sutton Coldfield

Thunder

Thunder, thunder
Is freezing cold
But not for people in the house.
Pouring heavily down
Heavier and heavier as we speak
Rain falls down.
People getting soaking wet outside
Others inside staying dry
I wish this thunder would go fast by.
Hail like ice blocks
You could not see a living thing in sight
It's true you know.

Toby Duckworth (9)
St Anne's Catholic Primary School, Sutton Coldfield

The Seasons

Lithe young lambs skip to and fro,
Over colourful flowers scattered low,
In blossoming trees birds sweetly sing,
Some of the pleasures from the season of spring.

The sun was like a ball of fire,
As it rose in the sky higher and higher,
Hear the children laugh and play,
On the hottest summer day.

Colourful leaves swirl to the ground,
The wind tosses them round and round,
Spiky shells cracked open wide,
Conker treasure deep inside.

Snow covers the barren ground,
Hungry birds fly round and round,
Cold and snowy, day after day,
I just hope spring is on its way.

Megan Humphrey (9)
St Anne's Catholic Primary School, Sutton Coldfield

The Seasons

Spring is when the flowers blossom
And baby lambs are born

Summer is when the sea is full
Of dolphins and fish

Autumn is when the sea
Is rough and cold

Winter is when we play
With the snow.

Joshua Walsh (8)
St Anne's Catholic Primary School, Sutton Coldfield

A Season Poem

Spring, spring, what a wonderful season it is,
When all the lambs come to play,
I love spring, the best time to have fun,
You need to go out in the garden.

Summer, summer, I love summer,
Planting flowers, oh what fun,
Playing with my rabbits, boing, boing, boing,
Going to the beach, have an ice cream.

Autumn, autumn, what a great season,
Time to go out and play in the leaves,
I'd better go out and help Dad rake up the leaves,
All the squirrels looking for nuts.

Winter, winter, what can I say?
You're cold, you strike me frozen,
I hate winter, you get me damp,
The only thing I like about you is *Christmas!*

Hannah Kelly (8)
St Anne's Catholic Primary School, Sutton Coldfield

Weather Poem

I love winter snow and frost
But best of all is making snowmen

I love spring when flowers grow
But best of all are daffodils

I love summer when ice creams sell
But best of all the summer sun

I love autumn because days are cold
But best of all the autumn leaves.

William O'Sullivan (8)
St Anne's Catholic Primary School, Sutton Coldfield

Seasonal Poem

Winter is fun, I love the snow,
Winter is my favourite season,
Frozen lakes twinkle brightly,
Misty fogs swirl through the air.

Spring chicks hatch in a nest,
Spring rain 'umbrellas up',
Pink blossom trees growing slowly,
I wish I could stay in spring forever.

Summer sweat, summer sun,
Bright, colourful, blue skies shimmer,
I love the beach and the sea,
I love suntans and ice cream.

Autumn leaves red and gold,
Crisp, sweep leaves fall
Bare trees sway from side to side
I love the wind breathing in my face.

Clare Horrocks (8)
St Anne's Catholic Primary School, Sutton Coldfield

Summer

Summer is the best
The sun is like a big ball in the sky
Leaving no shade behind
Melting ice creams
Sweating people
Making children come out and play
Summer is the time when people go on holiday
Summer's coming, people are going
September is coming, summer is going.

Philip Winters (9)
St Anne's Catholic Primary School, Sutton Coldfield

A Season Poem

S pring is great, it's not very cold at all,
P lants grow in all sorts of places,
R aining sometimes who cares,
I love spring,
N ever hot but warm,
G oing outside running about.

S ummer's great, run about, play all day,
U mbrella, you can throw it away,
M e and my friends come out to play,
M e and my friends come out to play,
E ating ice creams, yum, yum, yum,
R unning around, let's have some fun.

W inter's cold, very cold indeed,
I don't like the winter, it makes wobbly knees go very cold,
N ever hot like summer, never ever,
T he coldness makes my knees shiver,
E eating hot dinners with warm gravy,
R ivers frozen, poor fish.

Molly Love (8)
St Anne's Catholic Primary School, Sutton Coldfield

Summer Poem

S ummer's hot, really boiling,
U nusual birds flying past,
M aking dinner, eating outside,
M y birthday's today, I pray,
E very day I play outside,
R olling around the racing track.

I want to play outside forever,
S parrows peck seeds, seeds from my hand.

H ot days come and go,
O ver the hills I can see the rising sun,
T omorrow I will ride my bike.

Daniel Shephard (8)
St Anne's Catholic Primary School, Sutton Coldfield

Weather Poem

S ummer is sunny and hot,
U nusual for warm clothes,
M oon is nice and shiny at night,
M aybe we'll go to the beach?
E ating ice creams is fun,
R iding bikes makes me warm.

S pring is never hot but usually sunny,
P laying outside is really fun,
R aining is boring when you can't play out,
I nside isn't boring if you have some games,
N obody knows if it is a rainy day,
G enerally it is sunny in spring.

Harry Swift (8)
St Anne's Catholic Primary School, Sutton Coldfield

Spring Poem

S is for the sun coming out
P is for pink blossoms growing on trees
R is for sheep raising lambs
I is for ivy climbing trees
N is for naughty boys throwing stones
G is for growing all your flowers.

Adam Shephard (8)
St Anne's Catholic Primary School, Sutton Coldfield

Summer Poem

Summer is the best, in the sun and on the beach,
Relaxing and sunbathing is the best,
Having ice creams and getting tans and building sandcastles
And in the shade, but it is still the best.

Daniel Willcock (8)
St Anne's Catholic Primary School, Sutton Coldfield

Winter

I look outside and what do I see?
The sky swirling with bright white snowflakes,
I step outside and feel the cold on my face,
Freezing wet and cold day,
Bravely walking through the long narrow street,
Crunch, crunch, crunch.

I look outside and what do I see?
A blank piece of paper waiting to be drawn on,
Mum calls hurriedly,
Dad shouts loudly,
But I just sit quietly by the hot fire,
Eating warm bread and jam,
Looking at the swirling snowflakes.

I look outside and what do I see?
A funny-looking snowman in the blank snow,
Putting on woolly clothes,
I slowly creep downstairs,
Excitedly open the door,
Pretty snowflakes racing and fluttering about,
Sky grows pitch-black,
Time for bed.

Katie Byron (8)
St Anne's Catholic Primary School, Sutton Coldfield

Summer

S corching sun shows its light
U nder the sun people get a tan
M oonlight shines in the dark
M ost of the time I just run about like mad
E very day ice creams melt and dogs gobble them up
R ainy days will be here soon so we better go inside.

Jonathan Hobbs (9)
St Anne's Catholic Primary School, Sutton Coldfield

I Want A Pet

I want a pet,
That's big and strong,
A dog won't do,
His tail's too long!

I'll have a hamster,
Yes, that's alright,
No, that's no good,
He'll only play at night!

A big long snake,
To frighten Dad,
I'll have one of them,
No, he'll only go mad!

I don't want a cat,
A cow or a pig,
No, I don't want them!
I want one big!

I want a pet,
That's as strong as iron,
I know what I want!
A big strong *lion!*

Kim Delaney (9)
St Hubert's RC Primary School, Oldbury

My Nan's Garden

My nan's garden has ruby-red roses,
Makes lovely posies,
Daffodils playing their trumpets,
Bluebells tinkling and owls winking,
Blue tits feeding and the garden needs weeding,
But everything is just lovely,
In my nan's garden.

Sarah-Jane Smith (9)
St Hubert's RC Primary School, Oldbury

St Hubert's

St Hubert's is the place to be,
playing and sharing is what you see.
Bullying and fighting, we can't stand,
we make sure that they shake hands.
Teachers and dinner ladies they totally rule,
students and helpers are totally cool.

English, maths, science and art,
learn these subjects and you'll be smart.
When you're lonely or need time out,
go to a buddy and they'll sort you out.
You can join us and be in our team,
because working together is like a dream.

We go on school visits every fortnight,
gaze at the woodlands and look at the sight.
We travel on coaches and buses too,
they always look clean and brand new.
We remember our manners, please and thank you,
if anyone sneezes we say bless you.

We arrive in school for ten to nine,
everybody gets there on time.
Hooray, it's dinner time, we're ready to rock,
we've been out here since 12 o'clock.
It's five-past one, the whistle has gone,
now lessons begin for everyone.

School council, we get ideas from you,
making our school look better and brand new.
Singing songs about Jesus and love,
we know God's love is around and above.
3.30, it's time to go,
back home to our families who we love and know.

Zoe Morris (9)
St Hubert's RC Primary School, Oldbury

Four Seasons

Spring
Spring, spring let me think
I wish I could be bright pink

Summer
Summer, summer is so fine
I would call it so divine

Autumn
Autumn, autumn is so cold
Leaves are falling very bold

Winter
Winter, winter, frost and ice
I wish I could be like the mice

So here's the season very nice
Not very sunny with frost and ice.

Hannah Tilley (9)
St Hubert's RC Primary School, Oldbury

The Beach!

I am at the beach, where it's sunny as can be,
I am at the beach, where we can make castles every day,
I am at the beach, where I bathe till sunset
And where we can paddle in the sea.

I see at the beach, people swimming in the sea,
I see at the beach, the lifeboats out at sea,
I see at the beach, bathing in deckchairs
And people yachting out at sea.

I smell out at sea, the salty ocean air,
I smell out at sea, hot dogs from the stall,
I smell out at sea, the suncream over me,
I am at the beach where we can play *all day!*

Manjit Kaur Atkar (10)
St Hubert's RC Primary School, Oldbury

Mum And Dad

You are the best mum and dad
That any kid could ever have,
You give us toys and lots of love,
You're like an angel from up above,
Sometimes we fall out but that's OK,
Because we make up the very next day.

You are the best mum and dad
And as a kid would say you're simply bad,
Most of the adults are simply mad,
But oh no, no not my boxing dad,
Most of the women are so thick and dumb,
But oh no, no not my clever mum.

You are the best mum and dad,
For simply being my mum and dad,
Some kids would say that's not fair,
But you're the person that doesn't care,
My dad is unique with his cheeky smile,
He reminds me loads of a crocodile.

You are the best mum and dad,
You're always there, so I'm so glad,
Mum is unique with her fine looks,
I can't find the words in dictionaries or books,
But I say you're my mum and dad
And you're the best I could ever have.

Curtis Williams (11)
St Hubert's RC Primary School, Oldbury

Friend

If I could have a friend it would be someone like me
Someone kind and caring who never shouts at me
I would like them if they're never mean and never will be
I would not mind if they were a he

I would not like them if they never see me
I would not like it if we had a row
I want someone who I look up and see
Whenever I am happy to see them, I will give a bow

I would not like them if they always show off
I would not like it if they set me up
I would not like it if they said, 'Lay off'
I would not like it if they say, 'Pay off'

I would like it if they can trust me with their heart
I would like it if I can trust them too
I would like it if they are into art
I would like it if they will play when I have nothing to do

I would not like it if you hated me
I would not like it if they were boring sometimes
I would not like it if they say we weren't meant to be
I would not like it if they kept saying, 'What's the time?'

I would like it if we were best friends forever
I would like it if we didn't get in knots
I would like it if we were together forever
But maybe I won't have just one, I'll have lots.

Lisa Watson (9)
St Hubert's RC Primary School, Oldbury

My Pets

I have a dog,
Whose name is Izzy,
When she plays, she goes quite dizzy.

I have a cat,
Whose name is Mat,
When he plays, he plays with a hat.

I have a bird,
Whose name is Natasha,
When she flies, she's a bit of a crasher.

I have a snake,
Whose name is Flake,
He makes slime, that's what he makes.

I have a rabbit,
Whose name is Lucy,
When she drinks water, she likes it juicy.

All my pets are very snooty,
But one thing they have in common
Is they are all cutey.

Daniella Houten (8)
St Hubert's RC Primary School, Oldbury

Friends Forever

Friends are forever, friends are for life
Friends are like a little light
Friends make you laugh when they tell you their joke
Friends are with you all the way
Friends might do what you don't
Now if you do something your friends don't share your talent
If you see others falling out, help them too
Sometimes friends can cry, so help them through
Then I'm sure they will help you too!
But remember even if you have a best friend
Have other friends too
Friends are like family
So keep them with you!

Amy Guest (9)
St Hubert's RC Primary School, Oldbury

Planet Of My Own

If I had a planet of my own,
I'd never need to have a moan,
I could use anything as money,
Milk or nuts or even honey.

I would be the planets' ruler,
There would be no one else more cooler,
There would be mountains of Toblerones
And castles with turrets of ice cream cones.

I'd have games consoles and more,
Watching cable and films galore,
I'd have a planet with no pollution,
Electric cars would be the solution.

If people could see my planet now,
They would all shout, 'Brill!' and 'Wow!'

Fiona Fincher (10)
St Nicholas RC School, Sutton Coldfield

The Seasons

I love the spring, when birds are nesting,
No time for resting,
Winds are blowing, daffodils bowing,
The days grow longer, the sun grows stronger,
I love the spring.

I love the summer when the sun shines bright,
There's lots of sunshine, there's lots of light,
Long holidays and the games we play,
Don't let those memories go away,
I love the summer.

I love the autumn, when wind blows in my face,
Leaves of gold and brown, fall all over the place,
Berries, nuts and conkers, make you feel bonkers,
I love the autumn.

I love the winter, especially the snow,
Sledges racing down the hill as fast as they can go,
With rosy cheeks, it's time for tea,
When warmth and love wrap around me,
I love the winter.

Sophie Ruane (10)
St Nicholas RC School, Sutton Coldfield

Candle

At the darkness of the night
It shines so very bright
So people can see
If they are looking at me
The flame flickers
Like a pair of yellow knickers
When the light goes out
I have to shout
Because I'm scared of the dark.

Imogen Burns (7)
St Nicholas RC School, Sutton Coldfield

The Aardvark Love Story

I'm looking great, feeling ready to dance
I've got a heart-shaped box - inside are some ants
I'm going to see a girl who lives across town
But I'll have to wait till the sun goes down

I never go out in the day you see
For the dark of night is better for me
When the moon is up and shining bright
That's the best time - it's Valentine's night

My name is Arnie and love is my game
I'm going to Annie, that is her name
I'll hold her paw in the bright moonshine
Then ask her to be my valentine

If she says yes, I'll be a winner
And I'll pay big cash for a fancy termite dinner
Then we'll take a walk so you can see
Just how happy two aardvarks can be!

Natalie Port (11)
St Nicholas RC School, Sutton Coldfield

Snowflakes

White, delicate shapes
Individual, unique
Yet all so pretty
All so pure

Collecting in clusters
Glimmering in the dim light
Beautiful
Icy

But then too soon I think
A change in temperature
Means so little to us
Until the snowflakes melt.

Mary Leese (10)
St Nicholas RC School, Sutton Coldfield

School!

Nobody leave the room,
Everybody listen to me.
We had ten pairs of scissors at half-past two
And now there's only three.

Nobody leave the room,
Everybody listen to me,
There were forty pencils at half-past one
And now there's twenty-three.

Nobody leave the room,
Everybody listen to me,
We had five rubbers at half-past ten
And now there's only three.

Nobody leave the room,
Everybody listen to me,
My favourite pen has gone for a walk
And it's really not funny.

Everybody leave the room,
It's finally half-past three,
But Timmy stay back, write a hundred lines,
Car boot sales don't come free!

Charlotte Middleton (10)
St Nicholas RC School, Sutton Coldfield

Jealousy

Jealousy is green,
It smells like killing gas,
It looks like a green-eyed monster,
It sounds like fingers scraping down a blackboard,
It tastes like poison
And it feels like slug slime.

Paul McKenna-Manghra (11)
St Nicholas RC School, Sutton Coldfield

Sisters!

Sisters, sisters always fight
They punch and kick and squabble all night
They fight and argue as much as they can
It drives their mum mad . . . man oh man!

This just wouldn't do in my family
Cos my two sisters and I are as sweet as can be!
We chat, we smile, we laugh and have fun
And we love nothing better than to play in the sun

We read, we write, we sing and we dance
We care for each other and that's not just by chance!
We talk and we listen; we really get on well
My family is great, but *my sisters* are swell!

And at night when it's bedtime, the only fight we'll know
Is who's first to the bathroom and into whose bed we'll all go,
Cos our beds are all small and snugly and bright
But we don't care, we'll squeeze in, so no one is alone in the night

We hug, we cuddle, tell stories and giggle
And we sleep side by side with the odd little wriggle
We know we are lucky, thank God we've all got our health
So we're happy together with our little bit of wealth

So as you can see there's three sisters in my family
And we work very hard to keep us all safe and happy
We're not selfish or cruel or nasty or unwilling
We help and we love and of each other, we're always thinking!

When we're older and wiser and much smarter too
We all know already, what we're gonna do!
Cos we're gonna be pop stars, all of us three
And we'll be known in the world as the 'Sisters of Murphy'!

Catherine Murphy (11)
St Nicholas RC School, Sutton Coldfield

Loss

Ghostly howls rose from the wood,
Moonlight swept across the land,
The river hitting the breaking rock,
As the man watched and watched.

In his time, he saw,
The whistle of the bird and the blossomed trees,
The calm waters and the shining sun
And when he had cared for others.

Then a distant cry of help was called,
When the fresh breeze flew past,
When fire rose from a torch
And provided anger and hate.

But now, all there is,
Is the sobbing of the air and the falling of the tribes,
Abandoned mines and dusty gold,
All left quiet and still.

Dermot Rushe (10)
St Nicholas RC School, Sutton Coldfield

The Seasons

Spring is for flowers, blue, yellow and pink,
Nights get lighter and we get brighter.

Summer is for holidays, weeks off school,
Sunny weather, sunbathing and barbequing food.

Autumn is for leaves yellow, green and red,
Nights are getting darker, early to bed.

Winter is for snow, all shiny and white,
Winter is for Rudolph, with his nose so bright.

Gemma Byrne (11)
St Nicholas RC School, Sutton Coldfield

Christmas Tree

I look through the window and I see
A beautiful decorated Christmas tree
It had tinsel all colours, blue, green and gold
As I stood out in the freezing cold
With round baubles hanging down
And an angel with a crown
That's the best Christmas tree I ever saw
Apart from my own which I love even more.

Kaitlin Mills (11)
St Nicholas RC School, Sutton Coldfield

Football

F eet running everywhere
O ver goes the ball
O ver the net
T ime's up, half-time
B ack on the pitch
A big cross boys
L ovely footwork
L ovely shot, 'Goal!'

Libby Dorsett (7)
St Nicholas RC School, Sutton Coldfield

Colour

C olour is on everything
O ranges, shelves, books and rings
L ollipops, boxes and felt tips too
O h and everything, including you
U nder, over and everywhere
R attlesnakes and even a bear.

Ella McCabe (8)
St Nicholas RC School, Sutton Coldfield

In The Jungle

In the jungle,
Wild and free,
You will get to see
Snakes,
Slithering high and low,
In the trees,
On the ground below,
Spiders,
Crawling through hollow logs,
Over rocks
And scrambling through bushes,
Trees standing tall and straight,
Things that we should appreciate.

Megan McGovern (10)
St Nicholas RC School, Sutton Coldfield

Magical Music

M agical music drifts you away
U ntil someone takes it away
S o many beautiful tunes to hear
I n and out of my ear
C an I play the tooting flute? Merrily, merrily 'toot'.

Neva Kavanagh (8)
St Nicholas RC School, Sutton Coldfield

My Feelings

My anger is steaming up,
My jealousy is stirring,
My loneliness overwhelms me
And my fear is upon me.

Michael McKenna-Manghra (11)
St Nicholas RC School, Sutton Coldfield

Santa Claus

(Based on 'The Highwayman' by Alfred Noyes)

The snow was a glistening cover over the frozen land,
Icicles like daggers, ready to drop.
The evergreens were a brightness in the white wonderland
And Santa Claus came flying, flying, flying,
Santa Claus came flying to the orphanage roof

He'd a red and white hat on his forehead,
A lot of hair at his chin,
A coat of red cotton and fake polar bear skin
And he rode with a jewelled twinkle,
His blue eyes a-twinkle, his radiant smile a-twinkle,
Under the cold, cold sky.

Over the roof he crept and sneaked, in the dark night,
He looked through the windows and shutters,
But all the children were wrapped up tight,
He whistled a tune to himself, hummed while he crept,
Someone heard him, someone did hear him and up that child leapt.

The child watched him, pretending to be asleep,
While Santa crept, while Santa sneaked,
Santa had given out the presents, so he phoned Mrs Claus,
'I'll be home by morning light, watch for me at morning light,
Though the wind may bar my way,'
So he tugged at his reins and headed north.

Kyle Archer-Picknell (11)
St Nicholas RC School, Sutton Coldfield

My Dog

I have a dog, her name is Meg
And I have taught her how to beg
We go to the park, she has a very loud bark
She is black and white but she does not bite
She is quite small but she can fetch a ball.

Thomas Grant (9)
St Nicholas RC School, Sutton Coldfield

Winter

Winter's come, the frost is here,
I like it at this time of year.
I wish, I wish for snow to fall,
So I can build a snowman tall.
But all that falls is a few flakes,
A tiny snowman, that's all it makes,
That melts away,
Within a day.

My mum tells me that when she was small,
The snow, it used to fall and fall,
In big deep drifts to be cleared away,
Before you could go out for the day,
The gardens they were always white,
The snow would fall both day and night,
The snow would stay
For days and days.

I wish I lived back in those days!

James Maguire (10)
St Nicholas RC School, Sutton Coldfield

Sorrow

Sorrow is blue,
It looks like a dark cloud pushing the sun away,
Like a tree losing its last leaf.
It sounds like an echo in your ear,
Like a door slamming shut.
It feels like an icicle in your heart,
Like every light going out.
Sorrow is blue.

Natasha Gill (11)
St Nicholas RC School, Sutton Coldfield

Brothers!

Why can't you leave me alone?
Oh, don't have a moan.

Leave me alone today.
No, I can't play.

Why today of all days?
Why? Because Mum says.

Leave me alone and I'll be nice,
I'll give you one of my chocolate mice.

You know you're such a pain,
More horrid that that boy called Wayne.

What is more worse than mothers?

Brothers!

Jessica Dickens (10)
St Nicholas RC School, Sutton Coldfield

The Scary Surprise

The flames flicker
The night deepens
Something's moving
In the shadows
I opened the door
What's out there?
Is it a monster
Or maybe a lion?
Bang!
I ran up the stairs
There's a sound of footsteps
I went into the bedroom
I turned around
It's next-door's cat.

Rebecca Maher (10)
St Nicholas RC School, Sutton Coldfield

Custard Cream

Every night I have a nightmare
About thick and slimy custard cream
It boils over there and it boils over here
Hurrying down like a thick misty stream

But then suddenly there it came
Rushing like a hurricane
I hurried away but was too late
It covered me, it wasn't great

Then I saw a shadow
Lurking up the lake
He ran to me but then
I was in my room wide awake.

Alexander Hynes (10)
St Nicholas RC School, Sutton Coldfield

Sam From 'Lord Of The Rings'

Sam from 'Lord of the Rings'
Is good at a lot of things,
He's always nice and is a loyal friend
And never drives Frodo round the bend.

He is by far the best
And is better than all the rest.
He never gets very mad
Because he isn't very bad.

Sam has no fear
And loves drinking lots of beer,
Sam is trying to destroy a ring,
Which really is an evil thing.

James Heather (9)
St Nicholas RC School, Sutton Coldfield

Egypt Lost

Egypt, the land of many treasures,
Its wealth is hard to measure.

Once a country full of kings,
Pyramids full of diamond rings.

Dancing and singing in the temple,
The ancient Egyptians would assemble.

Today Egypt is not the same,
Although the temples still remain.

The people are poor with little to eat,
Working hard in all the heat.

Children begging in the road,
Donkeys carry a heavy load.

Where have all the treasures gone?
They have been stolen one by one.

Full of joy and full of sorrow,
But the sun will always shine tomorrow.

Georgia McCulloch (9)
St Nicholas RC School, Sutton Coldfield

Snow

I can feel it crunch beneath my feet,
I look around to see a great white sheet,
The trees are glistening and my nose runs cold,
I put my hat and gloves on, don't wait to be told.
Soft flakes are falling and robin hops across the sheet,
Small children laughing, their hats and scarves so neat,
Fingers and toes are growing numb, as I shape the icy mould,
A smiley face staring back at me, as I give my hand to hold.
Mixed feelings now the sun is out, it's come to end my play,
The watery sheet slips away, until the break of day.

Sian Hayward (9)
St Nicholas RC School, Sutton Coldfield

Spring

I know it's spring because the sun is shining brightly
And the birds sing tunefully early in the morning

I know it's spring because buds are coming out on the trees
And colourful pretty flowers sway in the breeze

I know it's spring because of the fresh smell of grass
After it has been cut and the sound of the noisy lawnmowers

I know it's spring because I can play outside on my swing
And feel the warm sunrays on my back
I can ride my bike and play tig with my friend

I know it's spring because all the children come outside and play
And I hear them laugh and see them run around
I can hear the music from the ice cream van

I know it's spring because I can see a bright blue sky
And the new green leaves on the trees
And everything comes to life.

Katie McHugh (9)
St Nicholas RC School, Sutton Coldfield

My Cat

I have a fat cat, extremely black
A dopey cat called Sophie
A cat that eats and sleeps all day
A cat that's always too tired to play
Since she was small, she's sat on the wall
To annoy the two dogs from next door
One day during May the dogs broke away
And she doesn't go there anymore
The cats in our street
They come around and try to meet
My pet and best friend called Sophie
I think she would play, maybe one day
But today I'm afraid she's too dopey!

Helena Spragg (9)
St Nicholas RC School, Sutton Coldfield

War

War after war, grave after grave,
Always arguing,
Never listening,
Why can't it stop?

Many wounded,
Many hurt,
Many killed,
Why can't it stop?

Families split,
Hearts broken,
Tears pour,
Why can't it stop?

Gunshot after gunshot, bomb after bomb,
Always fighting,
Never thinking,
Why can't it stop?

Many scared,
Many losses,
Much sadness,
Why can't it stop?

Lives ruined,
Terrible grief,
And all for what?
Why can't it stop?

Patrick Farrell (10)
St Nicholas RC School, Sutton Coldfield

Elephant Poem

The elephant walked to the water hole
Under a bed of stars
The night was as black as coal
You could see Venus, Jupiter and Mars
Deep into the night he stole
To the water hole

The elephant walked to the shade
Under a nearby tree
He looked and watched the footprints he made
And gazed at the faraway sea
Deep into the night he stole
To the water hole.

Chloe Hayes (10)
St Nicholas RC School, Sutton Coldfield

Feelings

Sometimes you feel happy,
Other times sad,
People can make you feel good,
They can make you feel bad,
We sometimes feel lively,
We sometimes feel tired,
We also get excited,
But then again we also get bored,
No matter how you feel,
Just remember you are always yourself
And always have someone to share your feelings with.

Georgina O'Sullivan (10)
St Nicholas RC School, Sutton Coldfield

Tiger, Tiger

Tiger, tiger, beast of fire,
Your coat full of fire,
How you burn bright,
In the mist of the night.

Tiger, tiger, king of the wild,
How you act in your wild way,
Your aggressive way,
As you kill each and every day.

Tiger, tiger, the one to kill,
Your sharp, razor claws ready to kill,
How you wait to pounce,
Then like a spring you uncoil.

Tiger, tiger, how you sleep,
How you curl up in your ball,
Your terror is gone,
Now we hear the pitter-patter of your cubs' tiny paws,
You tiger, tiger, have gone soft,
For you are the family man of your pack.

James Cahill (9)
St Nicholas RC School, Sutton Coldfield

Nonsense Poems

Hickory mickory mock
The elephant hit the clock
The clock chimed out
'Get off my snout'
Hickory mickory mock

Grumpy Humpty scowled at the floor
Grumpy Humpty slammed the front door
He drove down the road in a terrible rage
And everyone shouted, 'Start acting your age!'

Joseph Roberts (9)
St Nicholas RC School, Sutton Coldfield

Winter

Winter crisp, winter white
Winter in the twilight
Snowflakes falling in the night
Winter crisp, winter white

Winter crisp, winter white
Winter in the starlight
Snowflakes sparkle in the night
Winter crisp, winter white

Winter crisp, winter white
Winter in the sunlight
Snowflakes glisten in the day
Winter crisp, winter white

Winter crisp, winter white
Winter in the daylight
Snowflakes falling in the day
Winter crisp, winter white

Winter crisp, winter white
Winter in the dawn light
Snowfall fading, snowdrop waking
Winter away, spring on its way.

James Leese (9)
St Nicholas RC School, Sutton Coldfield

Pink Is . . .

P ink is a pig
I n its sty
N ow with its piglets
K nowing that people haven't seen her fly in the sky.

Sarah Cotter (9)
St Nicholas RC School, Sutton Coldfield

Smokey

Smokey is my guinea pig,
He jumps around his cage,
When he doesn't get his food
He shrieks out loud with rage.

His fur is grey, his eyes are black,
His nails are long and shiny,
He really is a fantastic pet,
Even though he is quite tiny.

When I get him out to play,
He runs right up my chest,
He makes himself quite comfortable
And loves my shoulder best.

He loves to nibble on my cheek
And also bite my ear,
And when I try to pull him off,
He pulls himself back near.

Kathryn Hoverd (9)
St Nicholas RC School, Sutton Coldfield

The Wind

Children shivered in their beds
As it howled through the trees

It strolled through the barren streets
Like a lost stranger searching for warmth

It sounded like a cackling witch in her cave
As it moved from house to house

It sang its mournful song
As it passed through the forests

It moved leaves across the town
Like helpless scurrying rats

Its touch went away
As the sun came up.

Eleanor Holloway (9)
St Nicholas RC School, Sutton Coldfield

Colours Of Life

Y is for yellow,
The colour of the deadly desert sun.
B is for blue,
The colour of loneliness and tears.
G is for green,
The colour of lush, healthy trees and plants.
R is for red,
The colour of anger and blood.
O is for orange,
The colour of a juicy, ripe fruit.
B is for brown,
The colour of Cadbury's mouth-watering milk chocolate.
P is for pink,
The colour of a sweet smelling rose.
B is for black,
The colour of the dead of night in winter.
G is for grey,
The colour of mouldy tombstones in a cold graveyard.
These are the colours of life,
The colours of the world.

Rosie Coles (11)
St Nicholas RC School, Sutton Coldfield

Rainbow Poem

R is for red like a warm fire
A is for amber that glows in the middle of the lights
which lets traffic pass by
I is for indigo that brings us joy and luck
N is for navy, the colour of my sweatshirt for school
B is for brown for the bricks that build a new home
O is for orange like the sun shining bright
W is for white that brings us peace.

Chelsey Rawlings (9)
St Nicholas RC School, Sutton Coldfield

My Computer

My computer is cool
My computer is great
I like it so much I want to celebrate

I love my computer, it makes me forget
When I'm stuck inside
And the weather is wet

My mum's worried I go on it too much
Sometimes she even threatens
To pull out the plug

When she won't let me go on it
I beg to her, please Mum, please
She says no
So I go on the PlayStation instead

My computer is cool
My computer is great
Living without it, I would hate.

Matthew Reilley (11)
St Nicholas RC School, Sutton Coldfield

The Great White Shark

The great white shark
King of the sea,
Great white shark
They really frighten me

Great white shark
Deadly as can be,
Great white shark
Four times the size of me

Great white shark
Has sharp deadly teeth
Great white shark
In the sea beneath.

Liam Manifold (9)
St Nicholas RC School, Sutton Coldfield

A Conversation With Myself

Hello, it's your conscience speaking
Just calling to say hi,
You know, if life's a game,
Then I don't want to play anymore,
You think you're winning,
But just then you get the 'go straight to jail' card,
Don't pass go, don't collect £200.

You know I've been watching us for a while now,
You never seem to care,
Lost your car, your girlfriend,
Even your house but now you're about to lose your life.

The world today is wrong,
You stand up for an old lady,
You get a bullet in your head,
So here's where it ends,
Goodbye old friend,
See you in Heaven, bang!

Jozef Raczka (11)
St Nicholas RC School, Sutton Coldfield

Wee Willy Winky

Wee Willy Winky jumping through the park
Up and down in his spotty gown
His teddy in his hand
He can hear the playing band
Under the open windows
Under the dripping locks
Are all the children in their beds
Now it is 9 o'clock.

Kerri Jenkins (7)
St Nicholas RC School, Sutton Coldfield

Pink

Pink is confident
It likes to show off!
Whenever you talk to it
It giggles and smiles

It tastes like laugher
It sounds like candyfloss
It looks like smiles from everyone

So whenever you touch it
It twirls and poses
So be lovingly around
Pink!

Ella McGrail (11)
St Nicholas RC School, Sutton Coldfield

Water

W e swim in it
A nd we live off it
T aps give it
E ating is less important that drinking it
R oll up to see what it is, it's . . . *water!*

Gregory Hayes (8)
St Nicholas RC School, Sutton Coldfield

Lighthouse

Big, strong lighthouse
Flashing in the sky
Lots of seagulls flapping by
Some people think it's old and sly
But to me it's my dream
Oh my, oh my.

Liberty Kilgallon (8)
St Nicholas RC School, Sutton Coldfield

Lighthouse

When it's night, it flashes bright
Stops the ships from crashing to bits
Lighthouse is the best
Because it saves the rest
Big lighthouse in the sky
Lots of seagulls flapping by
If it wasn't there ships would hit a rock
And the people would get a shock.

Kerry Gordon (8)
St Nicholas RC School, Sutton Coldfield

Night

The stars shine,
The moon is bright,
The sky is clear on a midsummer's night
The moon goes
And the sun appears
The grass is green
And badness disappears.

Miranda Burns (9)
St Nicholas RC School, Sutton Coldfield

Flowers

F lowers have got power
L ovely flowers are nice and kind
O nce I saw a flower with some power
W onderful flower red and white
E verywhere we look flowers are there
R ise flowers, rise in the sunlight.

Lauren Coles (7)
St Nicholas RC School, Sutton Coldfield

Ten Little Egyptians

(Based on 'Ten Little Schoolboys' by A A Milne)

Ten little Egyptians wasting time,
One got whipped and then there were nine.

Nine little Egyptians playing with their mates,
One went off and then there were eight.

Eight little Egyptians rising to Heaven,
One fell down and then there were seven.

Seven little Egyptians gathering sticks,
One dropped them all and then there were six.

Six little Egyptians giving high five,
One bent his finger back and then there were five.

Five little Egyptians playing with straws,
One lost it and then there were four.

Four little Egyptians playing on palm trees,
One fell off and then there were three.

Three little Egyptians climbing tombs,
One got caught and then there were two.

Two little Egyptians playing going, gone,
One had gone and then there was one.

One little Egyptian superhero,
One more gone and then there were zero.

Joseph Ward (8)
Tenterfields Primary School

Pyramids

P haraohs go in pyramids when they die
Y ellow is the colour of the pyramids
R ed pyramid was near the great tomb
A t Giza
M ummies were put
I n pyramids where there were trapdoors
D reams came true in the afterlife.

Molly Trudgill (7)
Tenterfields Primary School

Ten Little Egyptians

(Based on 'Ten Little Schoolboys' by A A Milne)

Ten little Egyptians all standing fine,
One fell over then there were nine.

Nine little Egyptians all with their mates,
One fell out then there were eight.

Eight little Egyptians all neat and clever,
One flew up to Heaven, then there were seven.

Seven little Egyptians fixing the pyramids,
One got bashed by a brick then there were six.

Six little Egyptians all messing with a hive,
A bee flew out and stung one then there were five.

Five little Egyptians were very poor,
One died and then there were four.

Four little Egyptians standing on a tree,
One fell off then there were three.

Three little Egyptians saying boo hoo,
One cried, then died, then there were two.

Two little Egyptians walking when the sun shone,
One was burnt then there was one.

Emma Hancox (7)
Tenterfields Primary School

Pyramids

P lenty of traps were hidden in pyramids
Y ou can guess why!
R obbers tried to steal
A ll the treasures
M illions of people built pyramids
I n Egypt, they were
D ifficult to build
S o they made ramps and used ropes.

Kieran Duff & Elliott Haydon (9)
Tenterfields Primary School

Ten Little Egyptians

(Inspired by 'Ten Little Schoolboys' by A A Milne)

Ten little Egyptians climbing up a vine,
One fell down and then there were nine.

Nine little Egyptians about to be late,
One tripped up and then there were eight.

Eight little Egyptians praying to Heaven,
One got pushed out and then there were seven.

Seven little Egyptians picking up sticks,
One got lost and then there were six.

Six little Egyptians about to eat chives,
One got murdered and then there were five.

Five little Egyptians going on a tour,
One didn't listen and then there were four.

Four little Egyptians found a palm tree,
One walked into it and then there were three.

Three little Egyptians caught the flu,
One died and then there were two.

Two little Egyptians standing where the sun shone,
One got burnt and then there was one.

Lars Silverwood (8)
Tenterfields Primary School

Pyramids

P yramids had gold tops,
Y ou can find these tombs today,
R obbers tried to get inside,
A lot of
M en worked as slaves
I n Egypt,
D ams could not be built,
S ome pyramids were smaller than others.

Jonathan Clews & Luke Owen (8)
Tenterfields Primary School

Ten Little Egyptians

(Inspired by 'Ten Little Schoolboys' by A A Milne)

Ten little Egyptians taking time
One got too hot and then there were nine
Nine little Egyptians about to be late
One got caught by a pharaoh and then there were eight
Eight little Egyptians praying to Heaven
One was sealed and then there were seven
Seven little Egyptians gathering sticks
One fell into the sand and then there were six
Six little Egyptians attacked by a chive
One ran into the Nile and then there were five
Five little Egyptians taking a tour
One didn't listen and then there were four
Four little Egyptians found a palm tree
One walked into it and then there were three
Three little Egyptians caught the flu
One was called to the pharaoh and then there were two
Two little Egyptians standing where the sun shone
One got burnt then there was one
One little Egyptian thought about the ones that had gone
He got whipped then there were none.

Daniel Scarrett (8)
Tenterfields Primary School

River Nile

R iver Nile
I s the longest river in the world,
V illagers need its water
E very day, Egyptians would die without the
R iver Nile.

N ets were used to catch fish,
I t is deep,
L ots of people came
E very year on holiday.

Lauren Hall & Abbey Parkes (8)
Tenterfields Primary School

Pyramids

P yramids were built thousands of
Y ears ago,
R osetta stone,
A llows you to read hieroglyphics,
M en made pyramids for the pharaoh
I n Egypt,
D ead pharaohs were buried inside,
S crolls were made out of papyrus.

Angela Eggleton & Jack Burkett (7)
Tenterfields Primary School

Pyramids

P haraohs
Y oung and old
R est in sarcophaguses when they die
A ll the
M ighty pharaohs wanted pyramid tombs
I n Giza is the world's biggest pyramid
D on't try to rob pyramids
S trange things might happen!

Nicholas Ward & William Connor (8)
Tenterfields Primary School

Pyramids

P yramids were used to bury the pharaohs
Y ou can see them in Egypt, the
R iver Nile flooded every year
A nd brought rich silt
M ummies were put in sarcophaguses
I nside the pyramids
D oors were sealed with wax
S ome of the pyramids are in ruins.

Jessica Waldron & Ellie Bayliss (7)
Tenterfields Primary School

Please Don't Smoke!

In my house I always breathe clean air,
As smoke, nicotine and fags are nowhere there,
Please don't smoke!

Smoking causes yellow teeth and bad breath,
Lung cancer, illness and death,
Please don't smoke!

Cigarettes influence young ladies
And damage your newborn babies,
Please don't smoke!

Want to live a long, happy life,
Children, husband or wife?
Then *please don't smoke!*

Laura Dobson (11)
Tenterfields Primary School

Stop Smoking

The world would be a better place
If people stopped smoking
There wouldn't be so many deaths
If people stopped smoking

Everyone's lungs would not go black
If people stopped smoking
No one would have heart problems
If people stopped smoking

There wouldn't be any lung cancer
If people stopped smoking
Everyone would breathe air again
If people stopped smoking.

Erandeep Fagura (10)
Tenterfields Primary School

Please Don't Smoke

Smoking can kill,
It blocks up your arteries,
So please don't smoke.

Smoking can start a fire,
It'll burn your furniture,
So please don't smoke.

You start by peer pressure
And end it by death,
So please don't smoke.

Smoking is addictive
And hard to stop,
So please don't smoke.

It may kill your children,
By damaging their lungs,
So please don't smoke.

Parents influence children,
They learn from you,
So please don't smoke.

Cigarettes are expensive,
All you do is burn your money,
So please don't smoke.

Smoking will give you asthma,
And also bad breath,
So please don't smoke.

I hope you've understood my poem,
So please don't smoke.

Anita Lateano (10)
Tenterfields Primary School

Ten Little Egyptians

(Inspired by 'Ten Little Schoolboys' by A A Milne)

Ten little Egyptians standing quiet and fine,
One fell in the Nile, then there were nine.

Nine little Egyptians all with their mates,
One fell out and then there were eight.

Eight little Egyptians all neat and clever,
One went up to Heaven, then there were seven.

Seven little Egyptians fixing the pyramids,
One got bashed with a brick, then there were six.

Six little Egyptians all alive,
One died and then there were five.

Five little Egyptians all scared of a claw,
One got beaten up and then there were four.

Four little Egyptians all of them were free,
One got a job instead and then there were three.

Three little Egyptians all with the flu,
One got sick and then there were two.

Two little Egyptians, nearly all of them have gone,
One got lost, then there was one.

One little Egyptian, everyone had gone,
He got lost and then there were none.

Chloe Taylor (7)
Tenterfields Primary School

River Nile

R iver Nile is the longest river in the world
I n it lurks lots of crocodiles
V illages of farmers in
E gypt need the
R iver Nile, it is very important

N ile has very clean water
I n it grows papyrus, ancient Egyptian
L ives were recorded on it
E vidence of pharaohs.

Lily Marsh (7)
Tenterfields Primary School

River Nile

R iver Nile is the longest river in the world,
I t flooded once a year,
V ital for the farmers,
E very year the water brought
R ich silt.

N ow they have a dam,
I t stopped the River Nile from flooding,
L ands stay dry because of the dam,
E verybody is safe now it has stopped.

Amy Hitchen (9)
Tenterfields Primary School

Mommy's Girl

She runs around from place to place
Putting a smile on her mother's face
She starts singing, it sounds like a bird
It was the most beautiful voice I've ever heard,
She goes in her room
She puts on a dress
She borrows some lipstick
To look her best
She looks out her window, she sees a tree
She puts on her apron
And says, 'Look at me!'
Her mum rushes upstairs
To see what she's done
She had drawn a picture of her and her mum.

Sophie Beckley (10)
Timbertree Primary School

Black Cat

Cat throws one sodden paw,
Over the wet and dirty floor.
Pads slowly inside the house,
Easily as silent as a mouse.
Walks up the rotten stairs,
Hasn't got any cares.
Creeps inside an ancient room,
Blending in with the misty gloom.
Knocking open a treasury box,
With all the stealth of a cunning fox,
Grabbing a single necklace in his mouth,
The cat streaks silently from the house.

Megan Woodward (10)
Timbertree Primary School